I0519203

Septuagint:

Ezra

Septuagint, Volume 10

SCRIPTURAL RESEARCH INSTITUTE
Published by Digital Ink Productions, 2024

Copyright

Septuagint: Ezra

Second edition. March 4, 2024

Copyright © 2024 Scriptural Research Institute.

ISBN: 978-1-998288-54-0

The Septuagint was translated into Greek at the Library of Alexandria between 250 and 132 BC.

This English translation was created by the Scriptural Research Institute in 2019 through 2023, primarily from the Codex Vaticanus. Additionally, the Leningrad Codex and Aleppo Codex of the Masoretic Text, and Dead Sea Scroll 4QEzra were used for comparative analysis.

The image used for the cover is an artistic reinterpretation of 'Battle of Salamis' by Wilhelm von Kaulbach, painted in 1868. The original painting is currently held by the Maximilianeum, in Munich.

Table of Contents

Forward.. 1

1st Ezra: Chapter 1.. 35

1st Ezra: Chapter 1 Notes.............................42

1st Ezra: Chapter 2..47

1st Ezra: Chapter 2 Notes.............................51

1st Ezra: Chapter 3..55

1st Ezra: Chapter 4..59

1st Ezra: Chapter 4 Notes.............................66

1st Ezra: Chapter 5..67

1st Ezra: Chapter 5 Notes.............................76

1st Ezra: Chapter 6..87

1st Ezra: Chapter 6 Notes.............................91

1st Ezra: Chapter 7..95

1st Ezra: Chapter 7 Notes.............................97

1st Ezra: Chapter 8..99

1st Ezra: Chapter 8 Notes........................... 109

1st Ezra: Chapter 9....................................... 111

TABLE OF CONTENTS

1st Ezra: Chapter 9 Notes.. 116

2nd Ezra: Chapter 1.. 121

2nd Ezra: Chapter 1 Notes.. 123

2nd Ezra: Chapter 2.. 129

2nd Ezra: Chapter 2 Notes.. 135

2nd Ezra: Chapter 3.. 140

2nd Ezra: Chapter 4.. 143

2nd Ezra: Chapter 4 Notes.. 146

2nd Ezra: Chapter 5.. 155

2nd Ezra: Chapter 5 Note... 158

2nd Ezra: Chapter 6.. 161

2nd Ezra: Chapter 6 Notes.. 164

2nd Ezra: Chapter 7.. 165

2nd Ezra: Chapter 7 Notes.. 168

2nd Ezra: Chapter 8.. 171

2nd Ezra: Chapter 8 Notes.. 175

2nd Ezra: Chapter 9.. 177

2nd Ezra: Chapter 9 Notes.. 180

2nd Ezra: Chapter 10.. 183

TABLE OF CONTENTS

2nd Ezra: Chapter 11.................189

2nd Ezra: Chapter 11 Notes.................191

2nd Ezra: Chapter 12.................195

2nd Ezra: Chapter 12 Notes.................198

2nd Ezra: Chapter 13.................201

2nd Ezra: Chapter 14.................205

2nd Ezra: Chapter 15.................209

2nd Ezra: Chapter 15 Notes.................212

2nd Ezra: Chapter 16.................213

2nd Ezra: Chapter 16 Notes.................216

2nd Ezra: Chapter 17.................217

2nd Ezra: Chapter 17 Notes.................222

2nd Ezra: Chapter 18.................225

2nd Ezra: Chapter 19.................229

2nd Ezra: Chapter 19 Notes.................235

2nd Ezra: Chapter 20.................239

2nd Ezra: Chapter 20 Notes.................242

2nd Ezra: Chapter 21.................245

2nd Ezra: Chapter 22.................249

TABLE OF CONTENTS

2nd Ezra: Chapter 22 Notes..253

2nd Ezra: Chapter 23..255

Septuagint Manuscripts..259

Alternative Translations..260

Dead Sea Scrolls..261

Also Available..262

Forward

In the mid 3rd century BC, King Ptolemy II Philadelphus of Egypt ordered a translation of the ancient Israelite scriptures for the Library of Alexandria, which resulted in the creation of the Septuagint. It is generally accepted that there were several versions of the ancient texts written in Canaanite dialects and Aramaic before the translation of the Septuagint. The two books of Ezra were translated into Greek and added to the Septuagint before 200 BC when a large number of refugees fled the ongoing wars in Judea and settled in Egypt.

The two books of Ezra were two different versions of the same basic story, however, 2nd Ezra appears to have been a massive redaction of 1st Ezra, in which even the god of Israel was changed. 2nd Ezra became the Masoretic text's version of Ezra, and by the year 100 AD, the Apocalypse of Ezra was in circulation as 3rd Ezra. The original 2nd Ezra was later divided into two books in Latin translations, making a total of four books of Ezra, although one was later renamed Nehemiah. This has created some confusion among Biblical Translators throughout the centuries.

The Septuagint's 1st and 2nd Ezra are thematically similar, telling the same story, however from two different points of view. They tell the story of the fall of Jerusalem, first to the Egyptians, and then the Babylonians, followed by Babylon's fall to the Persians, the Persians releasing the captured Judahites to return to Judah, and the rebuilding of the temple in Jerusalem. 1st Ezra was written from a non-religious viewpoint and repeatedly makes it clear that the author and various kings, all viewed the Lord as the Judahite version of other supreme gods, including the North Egyptian creator and sun god Atum, South Egyptian sun god Amen, and the Zoroastrian 'god of truth' and 'King of the Sky' Ahura Mazda. These views are inconsistent with the view of the Pharisees, which developed under the rule of the Hasmonean dynasty after Judea broke free from the rule of the Greeks, and the Lord became a separate god from all others.

Both the Greek translations of 1st and 2nd Ezra, and the Hebrew translation of Ezra-Nehemiah, contain relics of an Aramaic source texts, unfortunately, the Aramaic Books of Ezra and Nehemiah are lost. The differences in the surviving Aramaic words within Greek 1st Ezra, and Hebrew Ezra-Nehemiah indicate that the two versions of Ezra already existed in Aramaic. The differences between 2nd Ezra and Ezra-Nehemiah are minimal, and could be accounted for as scribal notes, along with the redaction of Simon the Zealot, who added the name Yahweh extensively to the ancient texts when he translated them into Hebrew. 1st Ezra, the less spiritual of the two versions of the Septuagint's Ezra, clearly dates to the Persian era, as it treats the Judahite Lord of the Temple in Jerusalem as another version of Ahura Mazda, the Zoroastrian God.

Several Zoroastrian titles of Ahura Mazda are applied to the Judahite Lord, including King of Truth, and King of the Sky. Letters from the Persian Kings Cyrus II, Artaxerxes I, and Darius II, as included in the book, all of which were closely associated with Zoroastrianism, yet, referred to the Judahite Lord using titles generally associated with Ahura Mazda. In the Greek 1st Ezra and 2nd Ezra, as well as the Hebrew Ezra-Nehemiah, the temple is described as being a Zoroastrian fire-temple, containing an eternal fire, which Nehemiah even referred to as burning naphtha, like the other fire-temples across the Persian Empire.

The majority of the Persian Era is missing from Rabbinical History, which skips 164 years of the Persian era. This era is known as the 'missing years,' as Rabbinical history places the destruction of King Solomon's Temple in 423 BC, while all other records state the Babylonians occupied Jerusalem and tore down the temple in 587 BC. Rabbinical history records that the Babylonian Empire fell around 70 years after the conquest of Jerusalem, which would be circa 353 BC, just 20 years before Alexander the Great conquered the

Persian Empire. Biblical history and the Babylonian Chronicles place the Babylonian conquest of Jerusalem in 587 BC, while the Battle of Opis, in which the Persians conquered the Babylonian Empire, is dated to 539 BC from multiple sources. This means the captives taken to Babylon were there for 48 years, not 70. The idea that the captives were in Babylonia for 70 years, stems from the prophet Jeremiah's prediction that they would be there for 70 years, however, this is not historically accurate.

The books of Ezra includes a Letter from Cyrus dated to the first year of his rule over Babylon, which therefore dates to 539 BC, however, the rest of the kings aren't always easy to distinguish from each other, as the Persian Empire had three kings named Darius, and four named Artaxerxes. The books of Ezra also describe several different groups of Judahites returning from Babylonia, and in 2nd Ezra and Masoretic Ezra-Nehemiah the stories repeat with different details, as once there must have been separate Aramaic books of Ezra and Nehemiah that contained different details.

The first group of Judahites to return from Babylonia was sent by Cyrus II after he conquered Babylon in 539 BC. They were led by Sheshbazzar, who was listed as the 'prince of Judah.' Sheshbazzar is not a Canaanite name, but a Babylonian name, šešab-sar (𒈾𒊓𒍝𒊬),

4

meaning 'sea orchard,' suggesting that this was literal translation of the name of the Canaanite goddess Ôṯtrt-Ym (𒀭𒌋𒆷𒅎), meaning Asherah of the Sea. This goddess later called Astarte (Ἀστάρτη) by the Greeks, had previously been banned by King Josiah, which would explain why the name was not translated by the Aramaic translators. It also indicates that this section of text originated in Neo-Babylonian cuneiform.

There are multiple references to the temple being destroyed again during Persian rule, and at least three temples must have been built under Persian rule if the records are correct. The first 'Second Temple,' Shesh-bazzar's Temple, appears to have been built as a Zoroastrian fire temple, shortly after the release of the Judahites in 539 BC, which is likely why there is virtually no record of it. In 1ˢᵗ Ezra, when Darius II restarted the work to rebuild the temple, he reported searching for Cyrus' commandments regarding the temple, and finding orders to build a temple where sacrifices would be made on 'eternal fire' (πυρὸσ ἐνδελεχοῦσ), which was a requirement of Zoroastrian temples, but never a requirement in the Torah. In 2ⁿᵈ Maccabees, the author writes a long preface to his abridged version of Jason of Cyrene's now lost five-volume version of Maccabees, in which he quotes obscure texts that do not seem to have survived to the present, including one which recorded:

Now, after many years, when it pleased God, Nehemiah was sent from the king of Persia, sent from the descendants of those priests that had hidden the fire. However, they told us they found no fire, but instead found thick water. He commanded them to draw it up and to bring it out, and when the sacrifices were prepared, Nehemiah commanded the priests to sprinkle the wood and that which laid on it with the water. When this was done, and the time came the sun rose and lit up the darkness a great fire was started, so that every man marveled.

The 'thick water' is later identified as Naphtha, a petroleum product used in Zoroastrian fire temples to maintain eternal fires. Waiting for dawn in order to light the fire is clearly a relic of sun worship, as King Josiah had banned praying to the east at dawn when he banned the worship of Shemesh, the ancient Canaanite sun god. If the quoted text of Nehemiah's actions is correct, he was a sun-worshiper, like many other ancient Israelites. King Josiah had attempted to ban the worship of Shemesh, the sun god, during his reforms of circa 625 BC, which was recorded in detail in the Septuagint's 4th Kingdoms (Masoretic Kings) chapter 23:

The king commanded Hilkiah the high priest, and the priests of the second order, and those who kept the door, to bring out of the temple of the Lord all the vessels that were made for Ba'al, and for Asherah, and all the army of Shamayim, and he burnt them outside of Jerusalem in the fields of Kidron, and took the ashes of them to the Temple of El. He burnt the sacred male prostitutes, whom the kings of Judah had appointed, and those burnt incense in the Bamahs and in the cities of Judah, and the places around Jerusalem, and those that burnt incense to Ba'al, Shemesh, Yarikh, the Zodiac, and the power of the armies of Shamayim.

He carried out the Asherah from the Temple of the Lord to the brook Kidron, burnt it at the brook Kidron, ground it to powder, and threw its powder on the sepulchers of the sons of the people. He pulled down the Palace of Qetesh that was by the Temple of the Lord, where the women wove tents for the Asherah. He brought up all the priests from the cities of Judah and defiled the Bamahs where the priests burnt incense, from Geba even to Beersheba.

He pulled down the house of the gates that were by the door of the gate of Joshua the ruler of the city, on a man's left hand at the gate of the city. The priests of the Bamahs did not go up to the altar of the Lord in Jerusalem, and they only ate leavened bread among their brothers. He defiled Tafeth which is in the valley of the sons of Hinns, constructed for a man to cause his son or his daughter to pass through the fire to Moloch. He burnt the horses which the king of Judah had given to Shemesh in the entrance of the Temple of the Lord, by the treasury of Nathan the king's eunuch, in the suburbs, and he burnt the Chariot of Shemesh with fire.

The altars that were on the roof of the upper room of

Ahaz, which the kings of Judah had made, and the altars that Manasseh had made in the two courts of the Temple of the Lord, the king pulled down and forcibly removed from there and threw their dust into the Brook of Kidron. The king defiled the temple that was near Jerusalem, on the right hand of the mountain of rubbish that King Solomon of Israel built to Astarte the abomination of the Sidonians, and to Chemosh the abomination of Moab, and to Moloch the abomination of the Ammonites. He broke in pieces the steles, completely destroyed the Asherah, and filled their places with the bones of men. Also, the high altar in the Temple of El, which had been built by Jeroboam the son of Nebat, who made Israel sin, even that high altar he tore down, and broke in pieces the stones of it, and reduced it to powder, and burnt the Asherah.

Josiah turned aside, and saw the tombs that were there in the city, and sent, and took the bones out of the tombs, and burnt them on the altar, and defiled it, following the word of the Lord which the prophet spoke...

The prophet guiding King Josiah was his father-in-law Jeremiah, a Yahwist prophet from the Levite city of Libnah in the Judahite-Edomite-Egyptian borderlands. Libnah had declared independence from Judah in the early 800s BC, at the same time as Edom over a religious dispute with the priesthood in Jerusalem. This appears to be a continuation of the dispute between the priests in Samaria and Jerusalem that led Samaria, Aram, and Hama to leave the union with Judah a couple of decades earlier.

The Edomites claimed that the Judahites had abandoned their god, and the rebellion in Libnah appears to have been for the same reason. The Judahites had responded by decimating Edom, but could not attack a Levite city, so Libnah and its hinterland became functionally independent until the time of King Hezekiah, a century later, who enacted the reforms the Levites in Libnah wanted, banning all gods other than their god Yahweh.

The Edomite god Qos (𐤒𐤅𐤎) appears to have been identical to Yahweh in every way other than his name, suggesting that the Edomites changed his name after the Judahites attacked them. The earliest records of the name Yahweh in relation to Canaan, are a reference to the land of the nomads of Yhwȧ (𓇌𓉔𓍯𓄿) from the Egyptian New Kingdom era, in the 13ᵗʰ century BC, when they are listed as one of six groups of shasu, meaning 'nomads,' living in the land of Edom. The shasu first appear in references to the enemies of Egypt east of the Jordan River in the 15ᵗʰ century BC, meaning if they were the Israelites, then the Septuagint's dating the Exodus to the mid-16ᵗʰ century BC makes sense. In any event, the Yhwȧ of the Edomites is generally considered a land, as it is referred to as the tȧ šȧsw Yhwȧ (𓇋𓈖𓉔𓍯𓄿), meaning 'land of the nomads of Yhwȧ.'

Pottery shards found at Kuntillet Ajrud in the Sinai desert, which date to approximately 800 BC, refer to

Yahweh as being both the god of Samaria and Teman, but not Judah or Jerusalem. Teman was an ancient Edomite clan and the name of one of their major settlements. The name Teman was used as a reference to all of Edom by Amos, Obadiah, Jeremiah, and Habakkuk, however, it was not their capital city, but rather the holy city of the god Qos, meaning the Yahweh of Teman from 800 BC, was known as Qos by 500 BC. This name shift took place under the influence of the Kushite Empire, which dominated Edom's international trade between 744 and 667 BC. The region had historically been dominated by Egyptian trade during the late Bronze Age, which began to reappear in the 10th century BC during the Libyan (22nd) dynasty. The Edomite and Libnahite rebellions during the 9th century BC must have been supported by the Egyptians, as Egypt gained strategic control over the Sinai peninsula and the Gulf of Aqaba. When the Kushites conquered the Libyan dynasty in 744 BC, they also organized an anti-Assyrian alliance of Canaanite states across southern Canaan, which included Samaria, Tyre, and Edom. Judah, which had historic animosity with both Samaria and Edom, instead allied with the Assyrians.

Under Kushite rule, the supreme god was Amen (𓇋𓏠𓈖𓏤), who formed the ruling triad of gods with his wife Mut (𓏏𓐝𓀭) and their son Khonsu (𓈖𓐍𓂋𓅃). Both the

Kushite King Amani (𓇳𓂋𓏥) and the Judahite King Amon (אָמוֹן) were named after Amen. Khonsu was the South Egyptian moon god, whose North Egyptian counterpart was Iåhw (𓇋𓂝𓎛𓅱), and Kushite counterpart was Khos (𓐍𓇳), which likely caused the shift of the Edomite name from Yhw (𐤉𐤄𐤅) to Qos (𐤒𐤅𐤔). The ancient Hurrian moon god of the original priesthood of Teman worshiped was known as ^{deity}Kushah (𒀭𒆪𒊭𒄴), and therefore the transition may have seemed like a restoration of the older pre-Israelite name of the god. The Edmonite Qos appears to have influenced the later Arabian storm god Quzah (قزح), suggesting he maintained Yahw's storm god attributes after the name change.

Nevertheless, after King Josiah was killed in battle against the Egyptians, King Necho II placed his son Jehoiakim on the throne of Judah, and Judah became a puppet state on the border of the Egyptian empire. King Jehoiakim appears to have rescinded his brother's reforms, and although the books of Ezra aren't clear on what exactly he did, do report it was evil, unlike Josiah's holy human sacrifices and sacred desecrating of corpses. 1st Ezra includes a very strange statement from King Necho II when King Josiah was preparing to attack his army:

> The king of Egypt sent a messenger to him, saying,

11

"What have I to do with you, king of Judea? I am not sent out from the Lord God against you, for my war is at the Euphrates, and now the Lord is with me! Yes, the Lord is with me pushing me forward. Leave from me, and do not be against the Lord."

King Necho II was a sun-worshiper, famous for building temples to Amen, the southern Egyptian sun god, and Atum, the northern Egyptian sun god. The god that sent him to make war against the Neo-Babylonians could not have been Josiah's God Yahweh, which is likely why Josiah didn't care what that god had to say. After turning Judah into a subject state, the first thing that Necho would have ordered was that worshiping his god was decriminalized. The Yahwist prophet Jeremiah, the new king's grandfather, was arrested and spent most of the following decade in the court prison as a heretic. His scribe Baruch, was a sun-worshiper and described the sun as being the Lord in the Septuagint's book of Baruch. Multiple ancient books of Baruch survive to the present, however, none were translated into Hebrew under the Hasmonean High Priest/Kings, and none are considered sacred by Jews.

During the rule of the Neo-Babylonian empire, the sun god Bel became the supreme god of the empire, and was then replaced by Ahura Mazda under Persian rule. Cyrus II was the first recorded Persian king to have an empty chariot drawn next to his own, so Ahura Mazda could accompany him into battle. His order to Sheshbazzar to build a fire temple for Ahura Mazda in Jerusalem would have been a wise strategic move, as it would have given his god a temple to live in near the frontier with Egypt, his new enemy, from which Ahura Mazda could protect the empire, and this is almost certainly the temple in Jerusalem that was using naphtha.

Cyrus II's heir, Cambyses II did conquer Egypt, Nubia, and Cyrenaica, however, was assassinated before he could launch his planned invasion of Carthage. The books of Ezra all include a letter sent by Tattenai, the governor of Syria and Phoenicia, which inquired about the temple that Zerubbabel and the Judahites were building in Jerusalem, along with a replying letter from King Darius confirming that Cyrus authorized the temple's construction, and Darius further ordering the governor of Syria and Phoenicia to assist. As this order to continue the rebuilding of the temple during Darius's reign was specifically mentioned as being after Artaxerxes stopped the work on the temple, the king in question has to be Darius II, Artaxerxes I's grandson. Darius II was the only Persian king named Darius who ruled for more than six years after a king named Artaxerxes.

Both 2nd Ezra and Masoretic Ezra-Nehemiah then mention in passing that starting in the first year of Ahasuerus (Ασουηρου / אֲחַשְׁוֵרוֹשׁ), the people of the land plotted to stop the construction of the temple in Jerusalem. Ahasuerus was the Aramaic version of 'Xerxes.' Xerxes (𒌋𒐑𒅁𒆜𒈫𒅁𒌋𒐑𒈫) is Old Iranian for 'ruling over heroes,' which was translated into Babylonian as Aḫšiyaršu (𒄩𒅁𒅔𒌋𒅁𒌋𒅁𒄩𒄑), and then transliterated into Aramaic and ultimately Hebrew as Achashverosh (אֲחַשְׁוֵרוֹשׁ). Xerxes I was Darius I's heir, who ruled between 486 and 465 BC. He is not mentioned again in any of the books of Ezra, so it must be concluded that he was not interested in whatever the people of the land were writing to him. He is generally viewed favorably in later Jewish literature, especially in the book of Esther, in which he married a Judahite woman named Esther.

All of the books of Ezra then include a letter from the officials of Coele-Syria and Phoenicia to a king named Artaxerxes, requesting he stop the Judahites from rebuilding the walls around the city, as they were a rebellious people. The king's replying letter is included as well, which orders the officials to stop the work in Jerusalem.

This verse is immediately after the verse in 2nd Ezra and Masoretic Ezra-Nehemiah that mentioned similar attempts during Xerxes' reign, implying it was Xerxes I's son Artaxerxes I, who reigned from 465 to 424 BC. Artaxerxes I fought a major rebellion in Egypt early in his reign, between 460 and 454 BC, which is likely when this order to stop rebuilding the walls of Jerusalem was issued. Between 460 and 454 BC, a Libyan prince named Inaros II launched a major, and almost successful insurrection in Egypt, capturing all of Egypt and Nubia south of Memphis, in modern Cairo. Inaros II's success was partly due to his alliance with the Athenians, who launched a major invasion of Anatolia at the same time as his insurrection, dividing the Persian forces. Ultimately the Persians defeated both the Egyptians and Athenian forces in Anatolia, however, the war took more than five years, and it seems likely that neither the officials in Syria and Phoenicia, nor the imperial government wanted a fortified city in Judea that could side with the Egyptians, and allow the Egyptian forces to move the battle from the Nile to the Levant.

The construction work in Jerusalem was reported as stopped until the second year of a king named Darius, which can only mean Darius II, as Darius I was Artaxerxes I's grandfather, and Darius III was the king defeated by Alexander the Great, who is not mentioned in the books of Ezra. Darius III had lost control of the western regions of his empire by his second year, and so the king who allowed the work to continue in Jerusalem after Artaxerxes I had stopped it, could only have been Darius II, whose second year was 421 BC.

In the second year of Darius II, 421 BC, Zerubbabel and Jesus ben Jehozadak led another group of Judahites to Jerusalem to rebuild the temple and the city walls. This suggests there were no city walls from before Artaxerxes I stopped the rebuilding of the city until Zerubbabel arrived in 421 BC. There are no records of what happened to Sheshbazzar's temple, however, the southern region of Judea had been occupied by Edomites in the interim, lands which Darius ordered returned to the Judahites. Artaxerxes I faced a major challenge to his dominion starting in his fifth year, when Egypt revolted, a revolt that took five years to suppress.

This still does not explain what happened to Shesh-bazzar's fire temple, however, the Aramaic language correspondence between the Israelite Temple in Elephantine and the Temple in Jerusalem may shed light on this. The Elephantine papyri was discovered in southern Egypt, near the ancient Persian fortress that once guarded the southern border of Egypt against a Kushite invasion, and spans approximately 495 to 399 BC. While the Temple in Elephantine was polytheist, and Yahw (𐤉𐤄𐤅) was worshiped along with his wife Anat (𐤏𐤍𐤕), as well as the sky god Bytalha (𐤁𐤉𐤕𐤀𐤋𐤄), the temple they were corresponding with in Jerusalem was monotheistic, with only Yahw documented as being worshiped there. This means that Yahw was considered the Israelite version of Ahura Mazda in Sheshbazzar's temple. The Elephantine papyri seem to agree with this, as in a letter called the Petition to Bagoas, who was the Persian governor of Egypt when the letter was written in 407 BC, they wrote:

> "Now our forefathers built this temple in the fortress of Elephantine back in the days of the kingdom of Egypt, and when Cambyses came to Egypt he found it built. They knocked down all the temples of the gods of Egypt, but no one did any damage to this temple."

Cambyses II was the son of, and successor to Cyrus II, who had sent Sheshbazzar to Jerusalem to build the temple. His reign was only a few years, however, in that time he conquered Egypt, Cyprus, and Cyrene, with the intent of marching his armies all the way to Carthage. However, he was assassinated in 522 BC, and a strange series of events took place that set Darius I on the throne later that year. Cambyses clearly viewed the Egyptian beliefs with contempt, and, as the Egyptian defenses were built to defend against invasion using large-scale ballistic weapons, reportedly placed dogs, cats, and sheep, among his troops rendering the Egyptian war machines useless. The Egyptians would not fire on the Persian armies as they did not want to anger the gods by killing the sacred animals, and therefore, the smaller Persian army was able to overwhelm the entire Egyptian kingdom in just a few months.

Cambyses spent the last three years of his life in North Africa, preparing for his invasion of Carthage, and is reported to have drained the coffers of the Egyptian temples, as well as passed laws to limit their wealth. Something happened in Persia that caused Cambyses to rapidly head back towards his homeland, however, he died en route, and his brother Bardiya briefly assumed the throne. A rebellion immediately broke out in Egypt, and apparently, the heavy taxation of the Egyptian temples was the main cause, which Darius I rescinded after he took the throne later that year. While there are no records of Cambyses actually destroying the temples in Egypt, that is likely what it felt like to the priests. The fact that he apparently left the Israelite temple in Elephantine alone suggests that like his father, he believed that Yahw was the Israelite version of Ahura Mazda.

The Petition to Bagoas, the Persian governor of Egypt in 407 BC was a request to provide funding to repair the Temple in Elephantine after an Egyptian mob had attacked it. This attack took place late in the reign of Darius II, the same king who had ordered the reconstruction of the temple in Jerusalem to be continued in 421 BC after he reported finding Cyrus II's orders from 539 BC. That temple, Zerubbabel's Temple, was reported in 1st Ezra chapter 7 to have been completed in the sixth year of Darius II, which was 417 BC. The damage to the temple in Elephantine in 407 BC, the seventeenth year of Darius II, was just three years before the Egyptians successfully revolted against Persian control in 404 BC, suggesting the Persians were already losing control in southern Egypt by 407 BC. It also shows the Egyptians viewed the Israelites and their gods as being loyal to the Persians.

When Artaxerxes I ordered the rebuilding of the temple and walls of Jerusalem to stop being rebuilt, it was almost certainly during the Egyptian revolt. As Cyrus did not send Sheshbazzar in 539 BC with orders to build walls, but a temple, it is likely the city did not have walls until Zerubbabel attempted to rebuild them under Artaxerxes I. After Cambyses conquered Egypt in 525 BC, Jerusalem would not have needed walls, as all the lands around Judea were part of the Persian Empire. Assuming the Egyptians felt the same way about the Israelites during their rebellion of 460 to 454 BC, during Artaxerxes I's reign, then it would have made sense to the Judahites to rebuild the walls of the city. Nevertheless, the letter to Artaxerxes claimed that they had laid the foundation of a temple, meaning Sheshbazzar's temple, which had been previously corresponding with the temple in Elephantine, had been destroyed or dismantled.

In 418 BC, year 5 of Darius II, while Zerubbabel was still building the second Second Temple, a priest named Hananiah sent a letter to the Israelite temple in Elephantine stating that King Darius had ordered the Judahites in Elephantine to observe Passover. The letter is known as the Passover Letter, and the author is accepted as Hananiah ben Zerubbabel, Zerubbabel's son. As the letter is sent claiming the authority of the king, it supports the claim in Ezra that Zerubbabel was a friend of the king's and also indicates that they remained in close contact as the temple was being built. King Darius ordering the Judahites at the garrison in Elephantine to observe Passover, which is clearly not a Zoroastrian custom indicates that the temple was no longer Zoroastrian, and that at least a Torah that included Exodus was being used in Zerubbabel's temple.

Based on the fact that the Elephantine letters only refer to Yahw being worshiped at the temple in Jerusalem, it is likely that the temple had a copy of Josiah's Torah, which would have included Cosmic Genesis, Exodus, Leviticus, and Numbers. Nevertheless, the temple in Elephantine did not, and Torahs do not appear to have been common at the time. The Samaritan priesthood likely had a different Torah including Exodus, Deuteronomy, and Joshua, however, other than the priests, it is unlikely anyone else had access to these Torahs. They were legal codes from countries that had ceased to exist centuries earlier, and if Ezra had not decided to publish his restored Torah, which combined the two, they may have disappeared entirely, like the Torah mentioned in the Wisdom of Solomon.

The identity of Zerubbabel has also caused some confusion over the millennia, as he is listed in the books of Ezra as 'the son of Shealtiel, of the house of David.' Shealtiel of the house of David is accepted as Shealtiel, the second exilarch of the Judahites in Babylon, who was freed from bondage by Amel-Marduk after his father Nebuchadnezzar II died in 562 BC. This would mean the person accompanying Jesus / Joshua is either Shealtiel's son, grandson, or male heir. The Masoretic book of Divrei-hayyamim (דִּבְרֵי־הַיָּמִים) further complicates this situation by reporting that this Zerubbabel was the son of Pediah, not Shealtiel, while the Septuagint's parallel verse in the Paralipomena reports he was the son (or male heir) of Shealtiel. To add to this, 1ˢᵗ Ezra deviates even further, by claiming it was not Zerubbabel who accompanied the High Priest Jesus / Joshua to Jerusalem, but Zerubbabel's son Jehoiakim.

Shealtiel was the protagonist, and possibly author, of the book known as the Judahite Apocalypse of Ezra, also called 3rd Ezra in some Christian Orthodox Bibles, 2nd Esdras in Catholic and some Protestant Bibles, and Ezra Sutuel (ዕዝራ ሱቱኤል) in Ethiopian Bibles. The Apocalypse prophesied that Jerusalem would be rebuilt by a Messiah named Jesus, who would then conquer the world. This Jesus was not the later Christian messiah, but a demigod who would yell fire and lightning at the world until it surrendered. The identification of 'Jesus' by name is taken by some as a sign of a Christian redactor, however, the prophecy was clearly not about the Christian messiah, and therefore there would have been no reason to add the name.

Given the correlation of a 'son of Shealtiel' and a high priest named Jesus / Joshua, it seems likely that this book was carried from Babylon to Jerusalem by the 'son of Shealtiel,' and his friend 'Jesus / Joshua ben Jehozadak,' in order to establish their authority over the government and temple via prophecy. If so, it explains who destroyed their temple, and why the Apocalypse of Ezra was later deemed to be heretical by Jews. If the 'son of Shealtiel' and Joshua ben Jehozadak were plotting against the Persian empire and planned to conquer the world, it was probably King Artaxerxes II who destroyed the city, in 380 BC, five years before Nehemiah traveled to

Jerusalem to rebuild the city. The 'son of Shealtiel' and Jesus ben Jehozadak would not have rebelled as long as King Darius II was alive, as he had given them secular authority over Jerusalem, however, his heir Artaxerxes II faced a major challenge to his assuming the kingship when Darius II died, and there was a Persian civil war. This seems to have inspired many rebellions across the empire, as well as the conflict against Sparta in the Corinthian War, between 396 and 387 BC. The destruction of Jerusalem is not explicitly recorded in the Persian records, however, must have happened shortly before Nehemiah traveled to Jerusalem in 385 BC, regal year 20 of Artaxerxes II.

As the 'son of Shealtiel' is generally assumed to be Zerubbabel, the son of the second Judahite exilarch Shealtiel, this would mean he could only have been sent to Jerusalem by Darius I, in 517 BC. According to conflicting sources, King Jeconiah was born in either 615 or 605 BC, and taken prisoner by the Babylonians in 597 BC. According to the Jehoiachin's Rations Tablets, discovered by archeologists excavating ancient Babylon, Jeconiah had sons by 592 BC, meaning his heir Shealtiel had already been born. While it is not clear when Shealtiel's son Zerubbabel was born, as this was his oldest son, and he was at least nominally wealthy, his firstborn son was likely born before he turned 25, meaning Zerubbabel would have been over 50 in Darius I's 5th regal year. If 1st Ezra is correct, that it was Zerubbabel's son Jehoiakim, he would have been much younger, likely under 30 in Darius I's second regal year.

However, in addition to the conflict within the text of the various Ezra and Nehemiah books, which claim that Artaxerxes stopped the rebuilding of Jerusalem before Darius restarted it, there is the fact that by Darius the first's second year, he was quickly becoming the strongest king that Persia ever had. Rebellions within Babylon and Egypt had been put down, and he was preparing to launch campaigns to expand the empire into Central Asia, and northern India. In 513 BC he launched an invasion of Europe, and marched his army through the Balkans and Ukraine, before building a series of forts along the Volga-Don portage. When he returned to Persia, the region of southern modern Ukraine was considered part of the Persian empire, a situation which continued for over 50 years. There simply was no reason to destroy Jerusalem under his rule, nor any records of disorder in the region.

When the work stoppage of Artaxerxes is added to the timeline, with Artaxerxes I being Darius I's grandson who reigned between 465 and 424 BC, then the King Darius who restarted the work in Jerusalem has to have been Darius II, who ruled between 423 and 404 BC. This clearly means that the 'son of Shealtiel' was a male heir and not the actual son of Shealtiel. This also explains why he was called the son of Pediah, which was another regal name, however, does not explain how the records got so confused. The confusion regarding whether it was Jehoiakim or Zerubbabel who traveled to Jerusalem with the High Priest Joshua, appears to be the result of this Jehoiakim being excised from the records as a false messiah, which would have happened if he led the Judahites in a failed rebellion. As something caused Jerusalem to be destroyed shortly before Nehemiah arrived in 385 BC, it seems likely that whoever was leading Jerusalem was allied to the Spartans and Egyptians in the Corinthian War.

1st Ezra is missing the Nehemiah content, and as such is a simpler version of the Book of Ezra, focusing on just Ezra's story. It may be one of the sources for 2nd Ezra, as the Ezra narratives are very similar, however, without the Nehemiah narrative, the chronology becomes impossible to understand, as the dating is based on the regal years of 'Artaxerxes,' yet the Persians had three kings named Artaxerxes. 2nd Ezra clarifies the situation, as Nehemiah was sent to Jerusalem in the 20th year of an Artaxerxes reign, and continued there until the 32nd year of that Artaxerxes. As this was after Artaxerxes I's grandson Darius II reopened the temple, and Artaxerxes

III only lived for 20 years, this had to be Artaxerxes II, who ruled between 404 and 358 BC.

Between the reigns of Darius II and Darius III, came the reigns of three kings named Artaxerxes, which seems to be the origin of the confusion over the timelines of Ezra and Nehemiah. Artaxerxes II reigned for 46 years between 404 and 358 BC. His son Artaxerxes III reigned for 20 years between 358 and 338 BC, and his son Artaxerxes IV reigned for 2 years between 338 and 336 BC. As the events found in the books of Ezra are specifically dated to the regal years 7, 20, and 32 of kings named Artaxerxes, Artaxerxes IV is not included in the books. Nehemiah dates his work to the years 20 and 32 of an Artaxerxes, which can only be Artaxerxes II, as Artaxerxes III only reigned for 20 years. Ezra dates his work to year 7 of an Artaxerxes, however, also refers to both Nehemiah and Nehemiah the younger as already present in Jerusalem when he arrived, which means his king was Artaxerxes III.

The era of the three latter Artaxerxes was a period of accelerating decline for the Persian Empire. When Darius II had died the Persians were fighting a rebellion in Egypt, which they lost soon after he died, initiating the last era of independence for ancient Egypt, which would last 60 years until Artaxerxes III would successfully reconquer the country just a decade before his own empire fell to the Macedonians. When Artaxerxes II assumed the throne after Darius II died, his brother Cyrus the Younger disputed his claim, initiating a brief civil war. The Spartans had supported Cyrus the Younger's claims, which led to the Corinthian War against Sparta, which lasted for 9 years between 396 and 387 BC. This war was very expensive for the Persians, who invested greatly in the Anti-Spartan coalition of Thebes, Athens, Corinth, and Argos. The main focus of the Corinthian War was to stop the expansion of Sparta, which had been conquering the Greek city-states and colonies. In 386 BC, Artaxerxes II suddenly changed his policies towards Sparta, betraying his Greek allies, by agreeing that the Spartans could conquer the Greek mainland, and in turn, the Spartans would end their occupation of Greek-speaking cities in Anatolia, which were returned to Persia. Artaxerxes II forced his former allies to accept the terms of the treaty, helping create the Spartan hegemony over Greece.

This sudden reversal of policy appears to have been a result of brewing revolts in the core of the empire, as, in 385 BC, Artaxerxes launched a campaign against the revolting Cadusians, in the region of modern northwest Iran. Artaxerxes II's 20th year was 384 BC, which was the year that Artaxerxes' cupbearer Nehemiah, requested to return to Jerusalem to rebuild the walls of the city. The Corinthian War was over, and by all accounts, Artaxerxes II had reunited his empire, and suppressed all the potential uprisings, except for Egypt, which had been lost twenty years earlier when he'd assumed the throne. Jerusalem was a major city along the land route from Egypt to Syria-Phoenicia, and Nehemiah must have known that the region could be invaded by the Egyptians in retaliation for any attempt by the Persians to reoccupy Egypt.

Ezra was also sent by a king named Artaxerxes, in his 7th regal year, meaning that this had to be Artaxerxes III, who in his 7th regal year, 351 BC, launched an invasion of Egypt, attempting to restore the break-away land to the Persian Empire, however, after a year of fighting the Persians were defeated by the Egyptians and their Greek mercenaries. After the Persian defeat in Egypt, Anatolia, Cyprus, and Phoenicia quickly declared independence. Notably, Jerusalem did not declare independence. The events described by Ezra, including the date and the xenophobia that Ezra enforced on the Judeans, fit well into this era, when the Persians were at war with the Egyptians, Greeks, and most of the peoples of Canaan, all of which Ezra had the Judeans evict from Judea. Artaxerxes spent the next few years brutally reoccupying the break-away regions, before launching another invasion of Egypt in 343 BC. Judeans are reported to have been taken captive in Phoenicia and relocated to Hyrcania, southeast of the Caspian Sea. Judeans were also relocated out of Egypt during the briefly restored Persian rule and were resettled in Babylonia and Hyrcania, suggesting that Artaxerxes III considered the Judeans to be loyal to the empire.

Ezra's commands, that all the Judean men of Israelite ancestry divorce their foreign wives and abandon their mixed-race children included many ethnic groups, including the Canaanites, Greeks, Perizzites, Jebusites, Moabites, Egyptians, and Edomites, but interestingly, the Persians, Medes, Arameans, Babylonians, and Assyrians, are not mentioned, and none of them were part of the rebellion during Artaxerxes III's reign. As Ezra claimed to have been dispatched by Artaxerxes, this appears to have been part of Artaxerxes III's attempts to restore order in the region. This segregating of the ethnic groups would have resulted in the majority of the unwanted foreign wives and mixed-race children being sold into slavery and would have alienated the Judeans from all of the neighboring ethnic groups, as well as the Greeks, who had backed the Egyptian revolt.

In 200 BC, the Greek Kingdom of Syria under the Seleucid Dynasty took Judea from Egypt and began an effort to Hellenize the Judeans, which included erecting a statue of Zeus in the Second Temple in Jerusalem and effectively banning traditional Judaism. This Hellenizing activity was partially successful, creating the Sadducee faction of Judaism, however, it also led to the Maccabean Revolt in 165 BC, which itself created the independent Kingdom of Judea. This Kingdom had a tenuous alliance with the Roman Republic until General Pompey conquered Syria into the Roman Republic in 69 BC. Pompey's goal was to liberate Greek-speaking communities in the Middle East that had fallen under the rule of non-Greeks when the Seleucids Syrian Empire had collapsed, and he carved up Judea, and Edom to the east, placing Greek-speaking cities under the protection of the Roman province of Syria. He also liberated several smaller communities that had been occupied by Judea, granting them self-government, including Ashdod, Yavne, Jaffa, Dora, Marissa, and Samaria.

A series of wars including both Julius Caesar's campaigns, and a Parthian invasion led to the weakening of the Hasmonean dynasty, and in 37 AD, the Roman Senate appointed Herod the Great as King of the Judeans. Herod's rule wasn't particularly popular, as he allowed the Romans to establish themselves within Judea, however, he did expand Judea, reintegrating the Greek and Samaritan cities, and annexing Galilee and Edom. When he died, his kingdom was divided between four successors, a situation that ended in 66 AD when the

Romans conquered the region. An uprising in 120 AD led to the Jews being exiled from Judea, and the region became a Greco-Roman colony. In the wake of the Jews, the Samaritans rose in numbers, along with the Christians once Christianity was legalized. Between 529 and 555 AD, the Samaritans revolted and were effectively annihilated by the Byzantine Empire.

The ancient documents found in the Caves in Qumran, more commonly called the Dead Sea Scrolls, span all of Judean history. Fragments of 2nd Ezra have been found in Hebrew, but not Greek, Canaanite (Samaritan, Judahite, or Edomite), or Aramaic, implying that this book was primarily used by the Pharisee sect of Judaism at the time, however, no copies of 1st Ezra have been found, even though it was generally considered the more authentic version in ancient times. The 1st century Jewish Historian Josephus quoted from it exclusively, ignoring 2nd Ezra entirely. With no copies found within the Dead Sea Scrolls, the Septuagint contains the oldest surviving version of 1st Ezra.

Outside of Judea, the Septuagint was the dominant form of Jewish scriptures across the Greek-speaking world, which by the beginning of the Christian era, extended from the Roman Empire in the west, to the Indo-Greek Kingdom in the east. Jewish traders had established small colonies along the trade routes of the

Red Sea and the Indian Ocean, reaching as far south as Yemen, and as far east as southern India, and these Judahites spoke Greek and used the Septuagint.

The earliest Christian Bibles, all used the Septuagint, however, by the 4th century some Christian scholars were debating whether they should retranslate the Old Testament from the version the Jews were using, and some even suggested using the Samaritan version. Both suggestions were generally dismissed as heretical, as Jesus and the Apostles had quoted from the Septuagint, even though they had access to the Hebrew version then in use. This argument held in the west until the Middle Ages when Catholic Bibles switched to the Masoretic Text. In the east, Orthodox Bibles continued to use the Septuagint, as they do today. To the south, the Ethiopian Tewahedo Church continued to use the Septuagint, and across Asia, the Thomas Christians and Nestorians continued to use the Septuagint. Only in Western Europe were the later Masoretic Text adopted, abandoning the more ancient Septuagint, on the assumption that the Judahites had copied their texts more faithfully than the Greeks had translated them. This assumption was carried forward into the Protestant Churches that broke off from the Catholic Church, and therefore almost all Protestant Bibles use the Masoretic Text for the basis of the Old Testament.

Unfortunately, this means that the earliest Christian writing was generally confusing and ignored by Protestants and Catholics. The earliest Christians of the first and second centuries quoted books that are no longer in the Bible, and as such, their writings are not always understood. Septuagint: Ezra is a 21st century translation aimed at correcting this problem.

One of the problems with academic translations of the Septuagint is the use of unfamiliar names or terms, as the Septuagint was in Greek, and therefore many names are unrecognizable to modern readers. This project uses the more commonly understood Hebrew-derived names instead of their Greek translations, such as Canaan instead of Chanaan, and Melchizedek instead of Melchisedec. Common modern names are also used instead of either Greek or Hebrew terms when geographical locations are known, such as the archaeological name Uruk instead of the Greek Orech, or the Hebrew Erech, and the archaeological term Sumer instead of Shinar or Senar. While this could be argued as not being a correct academic procedure, it does fulfill the goal of making the translation easy to read and understand.

1st Ezra: Chapter 1

Josiah held the feast of the Passover in Jerusalem to the Lord,[1] and offered the Passover on the fourteenth day of the first month, after organizing the priests into their daily schedules, being dressed in long robes in the Temple of the Lord. He spoke to the Levites, the holy ministers of Israel, saying that they should sanctify themselves to the Lord, to set the holy ark of the Lord in the house that King Solomon the son of David had built, and said, "You will no longer carry the ark on your shoulders, now, therefore, serve your Lord God,[2] and minister to his people Israel, and prepare your clans and families, as David the king of Israel prescribed, and according to the magnificence of Solomon his son, and standing in the temple according to the several dignities of the families of you the Levites, who minister in the presence of your brothers the Israelites. Offer the Passover in order, and make ready the sacrifices for your brothers, and keep the Passover according to the commandment of the Lord, which was given to Moses."

To the people that were found there, Josiah gave 30,000 lambs and kids, and three thousand calves. These things were given from the king's allowance as he had promised, to the people, to the priests, and the Levites. Hilkiah, Zachariah, and Syelus, the governors of the temple, gave to the priests for the Passover 2600 sheep, and 300 calves. Jeconiah, Shemaiah, Nethanel his brother,

Assabias, Uzziel, and Jehoiarib, captains over thousands, gave to the Levites for the Passover 5000 sheep, and 700 calves.

When these things were done, the priests and Levites, having the unleavened bread, stood in order according to the families, and according to the several dignities of their fathers, before the people, to offer to the Lord, as it is written in the book of Moses, and this they did in the morning. They roasted the Passover with fire, as the sacrifices are concerned, they soaked them in brass pots and pans with a good savor and set them before all the people. Afterward, they prepared for themselves and the priests their brothers, the sons of Aaron. For the priests offered the fat until night, and the Levites prepared for themselves, and the priests their brothers, the sons of Aaron.

The holy singers also, the sons of Asaph, were in their order, according to the appointment of David: Asaph, Zachariah, and Jeduthun, who was of the king's retinue. Moreover, the porters were at every gate, and it was not lawful for any to go from his ordinary service, for their brothers the Levites prepared for them. This was how the things that belonged to the sacrifices of the Lord were done on that day, that they might hold the Passover, and offer sacrifices on the altar of the Lord, according to the commandment of King Josiah.

So the Israelites which were present held the Passover at that time, and the feast of unleavened bread for seven days. Such a Passover was not kept in Israel since the time of the prophet Samuel. All the kings of Israel had never held a Passover like Josiah, and the priests, and the Levites, and the Judahites held, with all the Israelites that were found living at Jerusalem. In the eighteenth year of the reign of Josiah, this Passover was kept.

The actions of Josiah were upright before the Lord with a heart full of godliness. As for the things that happened in his time, they were written in earlier times, concerning those that sinned, and did wickedly against the Lord more than all people and kingdoms, and how they grieved him so much that the words of the Lord rose up against Israel. Now after all these acts of Josiah, Pharaoh the king of Egypt went to make war at Carchemish[3] on the Euphrates, and Josiah went out against him.

The king of Egypt sent a messenger to him, saying, "What have I to do with you, king of Judea? I am not sent out from the Lord God against you, for my war is at the Euphrates, and now the Lord is with me! Yes, the Lord is with me pushing me forward. Leave from me, and do not be against the Lord."[4]

How is it that Josiah did not turn back his chariot from him? He chose to fight with him, not regarding the words of the prophet Jeremiah spoken by the mouth of the Lord, but joined battle with him in the plain of Megiddo, and the princes came against King Josiah. Then the king said to his servants, "Carry me away out of the battle, as I am very weak."

Immediately, his servants carried him away from the battle, and when he climbed up on to his second chariot, he was taken back to Jerusalem, where he died and was buried in his father's sepulcher. In all Judea, they mourned for Josiah, even Jeremiah the prophet lamented for Josiah, and the noblemen and women mourned for him until today, and this was given out as an ordinance to be done continually in all the nation of Israel. These things are written in the book of the Chronicles of the Kings of Judah, and every one of the acts that Josiah did, and his glory, and his understanding in the law of the Lord, and the things that he had done before, and the things now recited, are reported in the book of the Kings of Israel and Judea.

The people took Jehoahaz, the son of Josiah, and made him king, replacing Josiah his father when he was 23 years old. He reigned in Judea and Jerusalem for three months, and then the king of Egypt deposed him from reigning in Jerusalem. He set a tax on the land of a hundred talents of silver and one talent of gold. The king of Egypt also made King Jehoiakim, his brother king of Judea and Jerusalem. He subjugated Jehoiakim and the nobles, but Zarion,[5] his brother, knew and sent him out of Egypt.

Jehoiakim was 25 years old when he was made a king in the land of Judea and Jerusalem, and he did evil before the Lord. Therefore, Nebuchadnezzar[6] the king of Babylon came up against him, and chained him with brass shackles, and took him into Babylon. Nebuchadnezzar, also took some of the holy vessels of the Lord, and carried them away, and set them in his temple in Babylon. But those things that are recorded of him, and his uncleanness and impiety, are written in the Chronicles of the Kings. Jehoiakim his son reigned in his place.[7]

He was eighteen years old when he was made king, and reigned only three months and ten days in Jerusalem, and did evil before the Lord. So after a year, Nebuchadnezzar sent messengers and had him taken to Babylon with the holy vessels of the Lord, and made Zedekiah king of Judea and Jerusalem when he was 21 years old, and he reigned 11 years. He also did evil in the sight of the Lord and did not care for the words that were told to him by the prophet Jeremiah from the mouth of the Lord. After that King Nebuchadnezzar had made him swear by the name of the Lord,[8] but he broke his word, and rebelled, and hardened his neck and heart, and transgressed the laws of the Lord God of Israel.

The governors of the people and the priests also did many things against the laws, and surpassed all the corruption of other nations, and defiled the Temple of the Lord, which was sanctified in Jerusalem. Nevertheless, the God of their fathers sent through his messenger[9] a call to return them, so he spared them and his tabernacle also. But they treated his messengers with derision when the Lord spoke to them, they mocked his prophets so much, that he became angry with his people for their great ungodliness, and commanded the kings of the Chaldeans to come up against them, who killed their young men with the sword, even within the boundaries of their holy temple, and spared neither young man nor woman, old man or child from among them.

He delivered all into their hands. They took all the holy vessels of the Lord, both great and small, with the vessels of the ark of God, and the king's treasures, and carried them away into Babylon. As for the Temple of the Lord, they burned it, and broke down the walls of Jerusalem, and set fire on her towers. As for her glorious things, they never ended until they had consumed and brought them all to nothing, and the people that were not murdered with swords they took to Babylon, to become their slaves their children's, until the Persians reigned, to fulfill the word of the Lord spoken by the mouth of Jeremiah, "Until the land had enjoyed her sabbaths, the whole time of her desolation will she rest, until the full term of seventy years."

1st Ezra: Chapter 1 Notes

1 Codex Vaticanus: tô cyriô (ⲧⲱⲕ Ⲩⲡⲓⲱ). Translation: the Lord

2 Codex Vaticanus: cyriô theô (Ⲕ Ⲩⲡⲓⲱⲟⲉⲱ). Translation: Lord God

The Septuagint's version of 1st Ezra was not redacted by Simon the Zealot, and therefore includes the term Lord God (Κυρίω Θεῶ), which, if correctly translated from the Aramaic source texts, would have read ådn hålhn (𐤉𐤍𐤋𐤍𐤕 𐤉𐤍𐤍), an Aramaic translation of the Canaanite ådn ålm (𐤉𐤋𐤟 𐤉𐤀𐤟). Ådn ålm was a Canaanite epithet for El, found in the Ugaritic Texts.

3 Codex Vaticanus: Charkamys (Ⲭ ⲁⲣⲕⲁⲙⲩⲥ)

Carchemish is an ancient city on the modern border of Syria and Turkey. It is the location where the Euphrates river gets the closest to the Mediterranean and was therefore important as an entrepot for the Mesopotamian cultures. Carchemish was a major city of commerce for Mitanni, Greek, and Neo-Assyrian Empires, existing from at least 1321 BC. This city was the site or staging ground of several major battles during the collapse of the Assyrian Empire, including the Battle of Megiddo circa 609 BC and the Battle of Carchemish circa 605 BC. This chapter is referencing the earlier Battle of Megiddo circa 609 BC when Pharaoh Necho II of Egypt sent his army to Carchemish to help restore the Assyrian Empire, which was being overrun by the Babylonians and their Mede,

Persian, and Scythian allies. At the time, Egypt and Judea were both supposed to be subjects of the Assyrian Empire, and Josiah's choice to attack the army of Necho II caused the Egyptians to stop and conquer Judah, which was then under the dominion of the Egyptian 26th Dynasty. Necho II send another army to Carchemish in 609 BC, but was unable to restore the Assyrian Empire, and the Neo-Assyrian Empire effectively ceased to exist.

4 King Nechbo II was a worshiper of Atum (𓇺𓏤𓏏𓏭), a fact established by the city he built being named 'Per-Temu Tjeku' (𓉐𓏏𓂋𓏏𓅓𓎼𓎡) which translates as 'The House of Atum in Tjeku.' This city was built between the Nile and Sinai Peninsula along the Mediterranean, where Necho II had ordered a canal to be dug that would link the Mediterranean and Red Seas. The fact that Ezra claimed that Necho II said he was sent by the Lord suggests that Ezra believed that the Lord was the Judahite version of Atum. There are several similarities between the Lord and Atum, both are the gods that created the world, and both are sky-gods. To those that worshiped him, Atum was both the starry sky, and the Sun-god.

According to rabbinical literature when Josiah's eldest son Jehoiakim was rebelling against the Lord he said, "I speak openly, all that God gives us is light, and this we no longer need, since we have a kind of gold that shines just like the light," which implies that he thought the Lord was the Sun.

Significantly, the cult-center of Atum in ancient times was the city of Heliopolis, where the Torah claimed that the Israelites were captive before Moses lead them out of Egypt. Heliopolis was called Iunu (𓉺𓏏) in ancient Egyptian, which was also the original name of the sky-god in Sumerian: Ān (✳), later known as Ilu (✳) in Akkadian, Ål (✳ / 𒀭 / 𐤋𐤀) in Canaanite, and Ålhå (𐡀𐡄𐡋𐡀) in Aramaic, all meaning 'God.' As this is also the name the burning-bush god of Moses originally identified himself as in the Septuagint: Ôn (Ὤν), it is entirely plausible that Ezra saw the Egyptian god Atum as a local variant of Ålhå / Ål / Ilu.

5 Codex Vaticanus: Zarion (ΖΑΡΙΟΝ)

6 Codex Vaticanus: Nabouchodonosor (ΝΑΒΟΥΧΟΔΟΝΟϹΟΡ)

This is accepted as a reference to Nebuchadnezzar II, king of the Neo-Babylonian Empire between 605 and 562 BC. Nebuchadnezzar II was the son of Nabopolassar, an Assyrian official who rebelled against Assyria in 626 BC. Nebuchadnezzar II was the chief architect of the Neo-Babylonian Empire, who in 605 BC, after taking the throne, launched an invasion of Assyria and Syria with his Median allies, and defeated the Assyrians and Egyptians, and incorporated Syria and Phoenicia into his Empire.

7 This is a noted deviation from the Masoretic Text which claimed that Jehoiakim's son was Jeconiah, however, the Septuagint consistently records two Jehoiakims (Ιωακιμ). The name Jeconiah (Ιεχονιας) does also show up in the Septuagint, however an unrelated noble. His name is recorded as Iaåúkinu (𒀀𒅀𒀪𒆪𒌑𒆠𒇷) in Babylonian records, however, this could be a transliteration of either Hebrew name.

8 As the supreme god of the Neo-Babylonian Empire was Marduk (𒀭𒀫𒌓), who was known as Bel (𒂗) meaning 'Lord,' this must be the god that Nebuchadnezzar II demanded Zedekiah swear by. If Ezra recorded this correctly, then Nebuchadnezzar II must have seen the Judahite Lord as the same god as Bel, whose name also means 'Lord.' As Marduk's name translates as ᶦˡᵘAmar-Utu (𒀭𒀫𒌓), meaning ᵈᵉⁱᵗʸCalf-Sun, it suggests that the Lord in question was a solar god, like the Egyptian Atum.

9 Codex Vaticanus: angelou (ⲀⲄⲄⲉⲗⲞⲨ). Translation: messenger

1st Ezra: Chapter 2

In the first year of King Cyrus[1] of the Persians, so that the word of the Lord might be accomplished, which he had promised through the words of Jeremiah, the Lord raised the spirit of King Cyrus of the Persians, and he proclaimed all through his kingdom, and also by writing, saying,

King Cyrus of the Persians commands:

The Lord of Israel, the highest god, has made me king of the whole world, and commanded me to build him a temple in Jerusalem in Judea. If therefore, there are any of you that are of his people, let his Lord God be with him, and let him return to Jerusalem that is in Judea and build the Temple of the Lord of Israel, for that Lord who lives in Jerusalem. Whoever then lives in the land, let them help those that are his neighbors, with gold, silver, gifts, horses, livestock, and other things, which have been set out by vow, for the Temple of the Lord in Jerusalem.[2]

Then the chief of the families of Judea and the tribe of Benjamin stood up, and the priests also, and the Levites, and all they whose mind the Lord had moved to go up, and to build a house for the Lord at Jerusalem. They who lived around them, helped them in all things with silver and gold, horses and livestock, and with very many gifts of a great number whose minds were stirred up to it. King Cyrus also brought out the holy vessels, which Nebuchadnezzar had taken away from Jerusalem, and had set up in his temple of idols.

Now, when King Cyrus of the Persians had brought them out, he delivered them to Mithridates[3] his treasurer, and through him, they were given to Sheshbazzar[4] the governor of Judea. This was the sum of them: 1000 cups of gold and 1000 of silver, 29 censers of silver, 30 vials of gold and 2410 of silver, and 1000 other vessels. All the vessels of gold and of silver, which were carried away, were 4569. These were brought back by Sheshbazzar, together with those who were captive in Babylon, to Jerusalem.

In the time of King Artaxerxes[5] of the Persians, Belemus, Mithridates, Tabeel, Rathumus, Beeltethmus, and Semellius the secretary, with others that were in commission with them, living in Samaria and other places, wrote the following letter to him, against those who lived in Judea and Jerusalem:

To King Artaxerxes our lord,

Your servants, Rathumus the chronicler, and Semellius the scribe, and the rest of their council, and the judges that are in Coele-Syria[6] and Phoenicia.[7] Let it be known to the Lord-of-Kings,[8] that the Judahites that were sent from you to us, having come into Jerusalem, that rebellious and wicked city, rebuild the marketplaces and repair the walls of it and lay the foundation of the temple. Now if this city and the walls are built up again, they will not only refuse to give tribute but also rebel against kings. As things about the temple are now in hand, we think it must not be neglected, but speak to our Lord-of-Kings, to the intent that, if it is your pleasure, it may be recorded in the books of your fathers. You will find in the chronicles what is written concerning these things and will understand that that city was rebellious, troubling both kings and cities. That the Judahites were rebellious, and always started wars, which caused this city to be made desolate. Therefore now we do declare to you, Lord-of-Kings, that if this city is built again, and the walls are rebuilt, you will from now on have no passage into Coele-Syria and Phoenicia.

Then the king wrote back again to Rathumus the chronicler, Beeltethmus, Semellius the scribe, and to the rest that was in commission, and residents in Samaria, Syria, and Phoenicia:

I have read the letter that you sent to me, and therefore I commanded to make a diligent search, and it has been found that that city was from the beginning, rebelling against kings. The men there were given to rebellion and war, and that mighty and fierce kings were in Jerusalem, who reigned and exacted tributes from Coele-Syria and Phoenicia. Now, therefore, I have commanded those men to stop rebuilding the city and ordered that there be no more done in it, and those wicked workers proceed no further to disturbance of the kings.

When King Artaxerxes' letters were read, Rathumus, Semellius the scribe, and the rest that were in commission with them rushed to Jerusalem with a squadron of cavalry and a horde of people in battle-formation and stopped the builders, and the building of the temple in Jerusalem stopped until the second year of the reign of King Darius[9] of the Persians.

1st Ezra: Chapter 2 Notes

1 Codex Vaticanus: Cyros (ⲔⲨⲢⲞⲤ). Translation: Cyrus

Cyrus II, also called Cyrus the Great, established the Achaemenid Dynasty, and the first Persian Empire. Between 559 and 530 he conquered an empire stretching from the Aegean Sea to the Indus River. Cyrus II is generally accepted as being a Zoroastrian, although this cannot be proven from archaeological evidence. He is believed to have also been the king that ordered the construction of the Avestan archives, and the writing down of the Avestan literature, which had previously only been sung or chanted, however, Alexander the Great's destruction of the archives may make it impossible to know who ordered its construction.

2 There are no references to King Cyrus II worshiping the Judahite Lord, or the Babylonian Bel, in the Persian records, and he was most-likely a Zoroastrian. From the time of Cyrus II until the time of Darius III, it was customary for an empty chariot to be drawn into battles for Ahura Mazda to ride in. If Cyrus II was a Zoroastrian, then this would imply that he considered the Lord to be Ahura Mazda, the Zoroastrian God, whose name translates as, 'Lord of Wisdom.' It would also mean that Ezra considered Ahura Mazda to be the Judahite Lord.

3 Codex Vaticanus: Mithridatê (ΜΙΘΡΙΔΑΤΗΙ). Translation: Mithridates

This is the Greek translation of the Persian name Mithradata (𐎷𐎰𐎼𐎭𐎠𐎫), which means 'Given by Mithra.'

4 Codex Vaticanus: Sanabassarou (ΣΑΝΑΒΑΣΣΑΡΟΥ)

• Leningrad Codex in Ezra section of Ezra-Nehemiah: Sheshebatzar (שֵׁשְׁבַּצַּר)

The name appears to be Babylonian šešab-sar ([illegible]), meaning 'sea orchard,' suggesting that this was literal translation of the name of the Canaanite goddess Ôṯtrt-Ym (𐎀𐎘𐎗𐎚𐎊𐎎), meaning Asherah of the Sea. This goddess later called Astarte (Ἀστάρτη) by the Greeks, and had previously been banned by King Josiah, which would explain why the name was not translated by the Aramaic translators. It also indicates that this section of text originated in Akkadian Cuneiform. The person being mentioned in unclear, although he is the person that receives the treasures from the Temple of the Lord in both versions of Ezra.

As Cyrus II released the Judahites, and did not attempt occupy Judah, it suggests that this was a Judahite prince that ruled between Cyrus' releasing the Judahites in 539 BC and Cambyses II's conquest of Southern Canaan in 526 BC. He disappeared from both Books of Ezra after receiving the treasures, which Zerubbabel later used to rebuild the temple. This has led some Christian groups to assume Sheshbazzar was another name for Zerubbabel, however, Zerubbabel was rebuilding the temple in 421 BC, during the reign of Darius II, more than a century after Sheshbazzar had been released by Cyrus II, making this explanation highly unlikely.

5 Codex Vaticanus: Artaxerxou (ΑΡΤΑΞΕΡΞΟΥ)

This is accepted as a reference to King Artaxerxes I, who ruled the Persian Empire between 465 and 424 BC.

6 Codex Vaticanus: Koíli Syría (ΚΟΙΛΗΙΣΥΡΙΑΙ)

Coele-Syria was the Greek name of the valley lying between the two mountain ranges, Lebanon and Anti-Lebanon, also called 'the Valley of Lebanon.'

7 Codex Vaticanus: Phoenicêi (ΦΟΙΝΙΚΗΙ)

Phoenicia is the ancient Greek name of coastal Lebanon and Syria.

8 Codex Vaticanus: cyriô basili (ΚΥΡΙΩΒΑΣΙΛΕΙ).
Translation: Lord of Kings

The early title the of kings of the Persian Empire was the 'Xash of kingdoms,' (𐎧𐏁𐎠𐎹𐎰𐎡𐎹𐎠𐎴𐎠𐎶), as they had many subservient Kings under them. It was later simplified to Xash (𐎧𐏁𐎠), and then developed into Shāh (𐭬𐭫𐭪𐭠). A modern equivalent would be Emperor, Czar, or Kaiser.

9 Codex Vaticanus: Dariou (ᴅᴀᴘᴇɪᴏʏ)

This is often assumed to be a reference to King Darius I, also called Darius the Great, who ruled the Persian Empire between 522 and 486 BC. However, as the Artaxerxes is listed as stopping the work on the temple, and Artaxerxes I ruled the Persian Empire between 465 and 424 BC, this must be a reference to Darius II, who ruled between 423 and 404 BC. Darius III had lost control of Judea to the armies of Alexander the Great by his second year, and could not have given the order. Additionally, the temple was rebuilt before Alexander's forces captured it, as High Priest Jaddua is recorded as taking him a copy of the book of Daniel to prove that the Judahites had been awaiting his forces to conquer the Persians.

1st Ezra: Chapter 3

When Darius reigned, he made a great feast for all his subjects and all his household and all the princes of Media and Persia, for all the governors and captains and lieutenants that were under him, from India to Ethiopia, from 127 provinces. When they had eaten and drank, were satisfied and had gone home, then King Darius went into his bedroom and slept, and soon after awoke.

Then three young men that were in the king's bodyguard, said one to another, "Let each of us speak a statement, and he that is cleverest, and whose statement will seem wiser than the others, King Darius will give great gifts and great things as a token of victory. He will be dressed in purple, and drink from gold, and sleep on gold, and have a chariot with bridles of gold, and a turban of fine linen, and a chain about his neck. He will sit next to Darius because of his wisdom, and will be called Darius' cousin."

Then everyone wrote his statement, sealed it, and laid it under King Darius's pillow, and said, "When the king rises, someone will give him the writings, and the king and the three princes of Persia will judge his statement the wisest, to him will the victory be given as was appointed.

The first wrote, "Wine is the strongest."

The second wrote, "The king is strongest."

The third wrote, "Women are strongest. But above all things, truth carries away the victory."

Now when the king had risen they took their writings and delivered them to him, so he read them.

He sent out for all the princes of Persia and Media, and the governors, and the captains, and the lieutenants, and the chief officers, and sat him down in the royal seat of judgment, and the writings were read before them. He said, "Call the young men, and they will speak their statement."

So they were called and came in, and he said to them, "Speak your mind concerning the writings."

Then the first began, who had spoken of the strength of wine. He said, "You men, how exceeding strong is wine? It causes all men to err who drink it! It makes the minds of king and the fatherless child the same, like the slave and the free man, and both the poor man and the rich man. It turns also every thought into humor and mirth so that a man remembers neither sorrow nor debt. It makes every heart rich so that a man remembers neither king nor governor, and it makes to speak all things by talents. When they are drinking they forget their love of both friends and brothers, and a little later draw their swords. When they are drunk from wine, they don't remember what they have done. You men, is not wine the strongest, that it makes us do this?"

When he had so spoken, he held his peace.

1st Ezra: Chapter 4

Then the second that had spoken of the strength of the king, said, "You men, don't men excel in strength that carries rule over sea and land and all things in them? Yet the king is more mighty, for he is the lord of all these things, and has dominion over them, and whatever he commands them they do. If he orders them to make war against one another, they do it. If he sends them out against the enemies, they go and break down mountain walls and towers. They kill and are slain, and do not disobey the king's commandments. If they are victorious, they bring all captives to the king as well the spoil, like all other things."

"Likewise, for those that are not soldiers, and have nothing to do with wars, but are farmers, when they have reaped that which they have sown, they bring it to the king and compel one another to pay tribute to the king. Yet, he is only one man. If he commands to kill, they kill. If he commands to spare, they spare. If he commands to destroy, they destroy. If he commands to make desolate, they make desolate. If he commands to build, they build. If he commands them to cut down, they cut down. If he commands to plant, they plant. So all his people and his armies obey him. Furthermore, when he lies down, he eats and drinks, and takes his rest, they keep watch over him and may not leave, or do his own business, or disobey him in anything. You men, how could the king not be mightiest, when he is obeyed in such a way?"

He stopped speaking, and then the third, who had spoken of women, and of the truth, (this was Zerubbabel,)[1] began to speak. "You men! It is not the great king, nor the multitude of men, nor is it wine, that defeats all. Who is it then that rules them? Who has the lordship over them? Are they not women? Women have named the king and all the people that rule in land and sea. From them, they came, and they raised those who planted the vineyards where the wine comes from. These also make garments for men, these bring glory to men, and without women men can't exist."

"Yes, and if men have gathered together gold and silver, or any other great thing, do they not love a woman which is magnificent in favor and beauty? Letting all those things go, do they not gape, and even with open mouth and stare at her, and have not all men more desire for her than for silver or gold, or any good thing whatever?"

"A man leaves his father who raised him and his own country, and clings to his wife. He seeks to spend his life with his wife and forgets father and mother, and country. By this also, you must know that women have dominion over you! Do you not labor and struggle, and give and bring all to the woman? Yes, a man takes his sword, and goes his way to rob and to steal, to sail on the sea and rivers, and looks on a lion, and goes in the darkness, and when he has stolen, spoiled, and robbed, he brings it to his love. Therefore, a man loves his wife better than his father or mother. Yes, some have lost their minds for women, and become slaves for their sake. Many also have perished, erred, and sinned, for women."

"Now, don't you believe me? Is the king not great in his power? Do all regions not fear to touch him? Yet, I did see him and Apame, the king's concubine, the daughter of the admirable Bartacus, sitting at the right hand of the king, take the crown from the king's head, and set it on her head! She also struck the king with her left hand. Yet, for all this the king gaped and stared at her with open mouth if she laughed at him, he laughed also, but if she took any displeasure at him, the king was quick to flatter, that she might be repulsed by him again. You men, how can it be any but women should be strongest, seeing they can do this?"

Then the king and the princes looked at one another, and he began to speak of the truth, "You men, are women not strong? Great is the earth, high is the sky, swift is the sun in his path, for he encircles the heavens around us, and follows his path to his own home in one day. Is he not greater who makes these things? Therefore great is the truth, and stronger than all things. All the earth calls on the truth, and the sky blesses it, all works shake and tremble at it, and with it is no unrighteous thing. Wine is wicked, the king is wicked, women are wicked, all the children of men are wicked, and such are all their wicked works, and there is no truth in them, in their unrighteousness also they will perish. As for the truth, it endures and is always strong. It lives and conquers forever. With her, there is no accepting of persons or rewards, instead, she does the things that are just, and refrains from all unjust and wicked things and all men do well like her works. In her judgment, there is no unrighteousness, and she is the strength, kingdom, power, and majesty, of all ages. Blessed is the God of Truth."[2]

With that, he held his peace, and all the people then shouted, "Great is the truth, and mighty above all things!"

Then said the king to him, "Ask what you will, more than is requested in the writing, and we'll give it to you, because you are found wisest, and you will sit next to me and will be called my cousin."

Then he replied to the king, "Remember your vow, which you have vowed to build Jerusalem, in the day when you came to your kingdom, to send away all the vessels that were taken away out of Jerusalem, which Cyrus set apart, when he vowed to destroy Babylon and to send them again there. You also have vowed to build up the temple, which the Edomites burned when Judea was made desolate by the Chaldeans. Now, Lord-of-Kings, this is that which I require, and which I desire of you, and this is the princely liberty proceeding from yourself. I desire therefore that you make good the vow, which from your mouth you have vowed to the King of the Sky."[3]

Then Darius the king stood up and kissed him, and wrote letters for him to all the treasurers and lieutenants and captains and governors, that they should safely convey on their way both him, and all those that go with him to build Jerusalem. He wrote letters also to the lieutenants that were in Coele-Syria and Phoenicia, and to those in Lebanon, that they should bring cedar wood from Lebanon to Jerusalem, and that they should build the city with him. Moreover, he wrote for all the Judahites that went out of his realm up into Judea, concerning their freedom, that no officer, ruler, lieutenant, or treasurer, should forcibly enter into their doors. That all the country which they hold should be free without tribute, and that the Edomites should return the villages of the Judahites which then they held. That there should be given annually twenty talents to the building of the temple, until the time that it was built. And another ten talents annually to maintain the burned offerings on the altar every day, as they had a commandment to offer seventeen. Also, that all those who left from Babylon to rebuild the city, should have liberty, as well as their descendants, and all the priests that went out

He also wrote concerning the orders and the priests' vestments in which they ministered. Likewise, for the orders of the Levites, to be given to them until the day that the temple was finished, and Jerusalem rebuilt. He commanded to give to all that maintained the city pensions and wages. He sent away also all the vessels from Babylon, that Cyrus had set apart, and all that Cyrus had given in commandment, the same he ordered also to be done, and sent to Jerusalem.

Now when this young man had gone out, he lifted his face to the sky towards Jerusalem, and praised the King of the Sky, saying, "From you comes victory, from you comes wisdom, and yours is the glory, and I am your servant. Blessed are you, who have given me wisdom, for to you I give thanks, the Lord of our fathers."

He took the letters, and went out, and came to Babylon, and told it all to his brothers. They praised the god of their fathers, because he had given them freedom and liberty to go and to rebuild Jerusalem and the temple which is called by his name, and they feasted with instruments of music and celebration for seven days.

1st Ezra: Chapter 4 Notes

1 Codex Vaticanus: Zorobabel (ΖΟΡΟΒΑΒΕΛ)

According to the Septuagint and Masoretic Text, he was the grandson of the Judahite King Jehoiakim II (Jeconiah), who then became the governor of the Persian province of Yehud Medinata, at the core of the old Kingdom of Judah.

2 Codex Vaticanus: theos tês alêthias (ΘΕΟϹΤΗϹ ΑΛΗΘΕΙΑϹ)

The King of Truth was a title for Ahura Mazda (𐬀𐬵𐬎𐬭𐬀 𐬨𐬀𐬰𐬛𐬂), the Zoroastrian God. He was also called Am (𐏈) in Persian, Åhwrmzd (𐡀𐡄𐡅𐡓𐡌𐡆𐡃) in Aramaic, and ^{ilu}Aḫurumaazda (𒀭𒀀𒄷𒊒𒈠𒀀𒊍𒁕) in Neo-Babylonian. The Old Persian deviation is likely influenced by the Sumerian word Ān (𒀭), originally meaning ‘god,’ however, treated as the name of the Babylonian sky god during the era.

3 Codex Vaticanus: basili tou Ouranou (ΒΑϹΙΛΕΙΤΟΥ ΟΥΡΑΝΟΥ)

The King of the Sky was a title for Ahura Mazda, later adopted by Jews and Christians as a title of God.

1st Ezra: Chapter 5

After this were the principal men of the families chosen according to their tribes, to return with their wives and sons and daughters, with their men-slaves and woman-slaves, and their livestock. Darius sent with them a thousand cavalry to escort them back to Jerusalem safely, and with musical instruments tabrets and flutes. All their brothers played, and he made them go up together with them. These are the names of the men who returned, according to their families among their tribes, after their several heads.

The priests, the sons of Phinehas the son of Aaron: Jesus the son of Jehozadak, the son of Seraiah, and Jehoiakim, the son of Zerubbabel, the son of Shealtiel,[1] of the house of David, out of the families of Pharez, of the tribe of Judah, who spoke wise statements before King Darius of Persia in the second year of his reign, in the month of Nisan, which is the first month.

These are those of Judah that returned from being captives, where they lived as strangers, who King Nebuchadnezzar of Babylon had taken away to Babylon. They returned to Jerusalem, and to the other parts of Judea, every man to his city, who came with Zerubbabel, Jesus, Nehemiah, and Zachariah, and Risaiou, Eninios, Mordecai, Beelsarou, Aspharasou, Boroliou, Roimou, and Baana, their guides.

The number of them from the nation, and their governors:

The sons of Pharez: 2172.

The sons of Asaph: 472.

The sons of Ares: 756.

The sons of Phaathmoab: 2812.

The sons of Elam: 1254.

The sons of Zatou: 945.

The sons of Chorbe: 705.

The sons of Bani: 648.

The sons of Bebai: 623.

The sons of Assad: 3222.

The sons of Adonikam: 667.

The sons of Bagoi: 2066.

The sons of Adinou: 454.

The sons of Atir Ezekiou: 92.

The sons of Kinal and Azetas 67.

The sons of Azourou: 432.

The sons of Hananiah: 101.

The sons of Arom: 32.

The sons of Bassai: 323.

The sons of Ariphou: 102.

The sons of Baitirous: 3005.

The sons of Bethlomon: 123.

Those of Netebas: 55.

Those of Enatou: 158.

Those of Bethsamos: 42.

Those of Kariathiarios: 25.

Those of Kapiras and Beeroth, 743.

Those of Chadiasai and Ammidioi: 422.

Those of Kiramas and Gabbis: 621.

Those of Makalon, 122.

Those of Baitolio: 52.

The sons of Niphis: 156.

The sons of Kalamo and Onous: 725.

The sons of Ierechou: 245.

The sons of Sanaas: 3330.

The priests: the sons of Ieddou, the son of Jesus among the sons of Anasib: 792.

The sons of Emmirou: 1052.

The sons of Phassourou: 1047.

The sons of Charmi: 1017.

The Levites: the sons of Jesus, Kadmiel, Bannou, and Soudiou: 74.

The holy singers: the sons of Asaph: 128.

The porters: the sons of Shallum, Atar, Tolman, Akoub, Atita, and Sobai, in all 139.

The servants of the temple: the sons of Isaf, Asipha, Tabaoth, Keras, Soua, Fadaiou, Labana, Aggaba, Akoud, Uta, Kittab, Agaba, Subai, Anan, Kathoua, Geddour, Iairou, Daisan, Noeba, Chaseba, Gazer, Oziou, Phinehas, Asara, Basthai, Asana, Maani, Naphisi, Akouph, Achiba, Asshur, Pharakim, Basaloth, Meedda, Koutha, Charea, Barchous, Serer, Thomoi, Nasi, and Atipha.

The sons of the servants of Solomon: the sons of Assafioth, Pharida, Ieili, Lozon, Isdail, Saphythi, Hagia, Phakareth, Sabii, Sarothie, Masias, Gas, Addous, Soubas, Apherra, Barodis, Saphat, and Amon. All the ministers of the temple, and the sons of the servants of Solomon were 372.

These returned from Tel Melach[2] and Tel Charasha,[3] under the leadership of Charaath,[4] Adan,[5] and Amar.[6] These could not show their families, and ancestry, or how they were of Israel. The sons of Delaiah, Tobiah,[7] and Nekoda were 652.

Of the priests that usurped the office, these of the priesthood were not found: the son of Habaiah, the son of Koz, and the son of Ioddous[8] who married Aygian,[9] a woman from the daughters of Barzillai,[10] and took his name. When the genealogy of these men was searched for in the register and was not found, they were removed from executing the office of the priesthood. Nehemiah and the military commander[11] said to them, that they should not be partakers of the holy things, until the rising of one dressed as a high priest came and stated the truth.[12]

Those twelve years old and upward from Israel, beside men-slaves and women-slaves, were 42,360. Their boys and girls were 7337, and the singing men and singing women were 245. There were also 435 camels, 7036 horses, 245 mules, and 5525 animals used to the yoke.

Some of the leaders of their families, when they came to the Temple of God in Jerusalem, vowed to rebuild the temple again in his own place according to their ability, and to give in to the holy treasury of the works a thousand things of gold, five thousand of silver, and a hundred priestly vestments. So the priests and the

Levites and the people lived in Jerusalem, and in the country, the singers also and the porters, and all Israel in their villages.

When the seventh month was at hand, and when the Israelites were, every man in his place, they came all together with one consent into the open place of the first gate which is towards the east. Then Jesus the son of Jehozadak stood up, and his brothers the priests and Zerubbabel the son of Shealtiel, and his brothers, and prepared the altar of the God in Israel, to offer burned sacrifices on it, following as it is commanded in the book of Moses the prophet. There were gathered with them out of the other nations of the land, and they erected the altar in his place, because all the nations of the land were at enmity with them, and oppressed them, and they offered sacrifices according to the time, and burned offerings to the Lord, both morning and evening. Also, they held the feast of tabernacles, as it is commanded in the law, and offered sacrifices daily, as was demanded. After that, the continual oblations, and the sacrifice of the sabbaths, and of the new moons, and all holy feasts. All they who had made any vow to God began to offer sacrifices to God from the first day of the seventh month, although the Temple of the Lord was not yet built.

They gave the masons and carpenters money, meat, and drink, with joy. To those from Sidon and Tyre, they gave orders that they should bring cedar trees from Lebanon, which should be brought by barges to the harbor of Jaffa, following that which was commanded by King Cyrus II of the Persians.

In the second year and second month after his arrival at the Temple of God at Jerusalem, Zerubbabel the son of Shealtiel, Jesus the son of Jehozadak, and their brothers, and the priests, and the Levites, and all those who had come to Jerusalem out of the captivity. They laid the foundation of the Temple of God on the first day of the second month, in the second year after they had come to Judea and Jerusalem. They appointed the Levites from twenty years old over the works of the Lord. Then Jesus stood up, and his sons and brothers, and Kadmiel his brother, and his son Jesus, with the sons of Joda, the son of Eliadoun, with their sons and brothers, all Levites, with one accord setters forward of the business, laboring to advance the works in the Temple of God. So the workmen built the Temple of the Lord.

The priests stood arrayed in their vestments with musical instruments and trumpets, and the Levites the sons of Asaph had cymbals and sang songs of thanksgiving, and praised the Lord, following that which King David of Israel had commanded. They sang with loud voices songs to the praise of the Lord because his mercy and glory are forever in all Israel. All the people sounded trumpets, and shouted with a loud voice, singing songs of thanksgiving to the Lord for the erection of the Temple of the Lord. Also of the priests and Levites, and the chief of their families, the elders who had seen the former temple came to the building of this with weeping and great crying, many with trumpets and joy shouted with loud voices, so that the trumpets might not be heard for the weeping of the people, yet the multitude sounded so marvelous that it was heard far away.

When the enemies of the tribe of Judah and Benjamin heard it, they came to know what that noise of trumpets should mean. They understood that those that were captives have built the temple to the Lord God of Israel. So they went to Zerubbabel and Jesus, and the chief of the families, and said to them, "We will build together with you. For we, like you, obey the Lord and sacrifice to him from the days of King Esarhaddon[13] of the Assyrians, who brought us here."

Zerubbabel and Jesus and the chief of the families of Israel said to them, "It is not for us and you to build together a Temple to the Lord God. We alone will build to the Lord of Israel, as King Cyrus of the Persians has commanded us."

But the heathens of the land, lying heavy in the inhabitants of Judea, and holding them captive, slowed their building. By their secret plots, and popular persuasions and commotions, they stopped the finishing of the building all the time that King Cyrus lived, so they were stopped from building until the second year of the reign of Darius.[14]

1st Ezra: Chapter 5 Notes

1 Codex Vaticanus: Iôacim o tou Zorobabel tou Salathiêl (ΙѠΑΚΙΜ Ο ΤΟΥ ΖΟΡΟΒΑΒΕΛ ΤΟΥ ϹΑΛΛΘΙΗΛ). Translation: Iôacim of the Zorobabel of Salathiêl

• Codex Vaticanus in 2nd Ezra: Zorobabel tou Salathiêl (ΖΟΡΟΒΑΒΕΛ Ο ΤΟΥ ϹΑΛΛΘΙΗΛ). Translation: Zorobabel of Salathiêl

• Leningrad Codex in Ezra section of Ezra-Nehemiah: Zerubbavel ben-She'alti'el (זְרֻבָּבֶל בֶּן־שְׁאַלְתִּיאֵל). Translation: Zorobabel of Salathiêl

• Leningrad Codex in Nehemiah section of Ezra-Nehemiah: Zerubbavel ben-She'alti'el (זְרֻבָּבֶל בֶּן־שְׁאַלְתִּיאֵל). Translation: Zorobabel of Salathiêl

1st Ezra and 2nd Ezra deviate regarding who this was. 1st Ezra lists it as Iôacim, a transliteration of Jehoiakim (יְהוֹיָקִים), the son of Zerubbabel, while 2nd Ezra, the Masoretic Erza-Nehemah, and the Targums all claim it was Zerubbabel himself who accompanied Jesus / Joshua. The Masoretic book of Divrei-hayyamim (דִּבְרֵי־הַיָּמִים) further complicates this situation by reporting that this Zerubbabel was the son of Pediah, not Shealtiel, while the Septuagint's parallel verse in the Paralipomena reports he was the son (or male heir) of Shealtiel.

Shealtiel of the house of David is accepted as Shealtiel, the second exilarch of the Judahites in Babylon, who was freed from bondage by Amel-Marduk after his father Nebuchadnezzar II died in 562 BC. This would mean the person accompanying Jesus / Joshua is either Shealtiel's son, grandson, or male heir. The Masoretic book of Divrei-hayyamim (דִּבְרֵי־הַיָּמִים) further complicates this situation by reporting that this Zerubbabel was the son of Pediah, not Shealtiel, while the Septuagint's parallel verse in the Paralipomena reports he was the son (or male heir) of Shealtiel. To add to this, 1st Ezra deviates even further, by claiming it was not Zerubbabel who accompanied the High Priest Jesus / Joshua to Jerusalem, but Zerubbabel's son Jehoiakim.

Shealtiel was the protagonist, and possibly author, of the book known as the Judahite Apocalypse of Ezra, also called 3rd Ezra in some Christian Orthodox bibles, 2nd Esdras in Catholic and some Protestant bibles, and Ezra Sutuel (ዕዝራ ሱቱኤል) in Ethiopian bibles. The Apocalypse prophesied that Jerusalem would be rebuilt by a Messiah named Jesus, who would then conquer the world. This Jesus was not the later Christian messiah, but a demigod who would yell fire and lightning at the world until it surrendered. The identification of 'Jesus' by name is taken by some as a sign of a Christian redactor, however, the prophecy was clearly not about the Christian messiah, and therefore there woulcorrelationd have been no reason to add the name.

Given the correlation of a 'son of Shealtiel' and a high priest named Jesus / Joshua, it seems likely that this book was carried from Babylon to Jerusalem by the 'son of Shealtiel,' and his friend 'Jesus / Joshua ben Jehozadak,' in order to establish their authority over the government and temple via prophesy. If so, it explains who destroyed their temple, and why the Apocalypse of Ezra was later deemed to be heretical by Jews. If the 'son of Shealtiel' and Joshua ben Jehozadak were plotting against the Persian empire and planned to conquer the world, it was probably King Artaxerxes II who destroyed the city, in 380 BC, five years before Nehemiah traveled to Jerusalem to rebuild the city. The 'son of Shealtiel' and Jesus ben Jehozadak would not have rebelled as long as King Darius II was alive, as he had given them secular authority over Jerusalem, however, his heir Artaxerxes II faced a major challenge to his assuming the kingship when Darius II died, and there was a Persian civil war. This seems to have inspired many rebellions across the empire, including a rebellion in Phoenicia in 380 BC. The destruction of Jerusalem is not explicitly recorded in the Persian records, however, must have happened shortly before Nehemiah traveled to Jerusalem in 385 BC, regal year 20 of Artaxerxes II.

As the 'son of Shealtiel' is generally assumed to be Zerubbabel, son of the second Judahite exilarch Shealtiel, this would mean he could only have been sent to Jerusalem by Darius I, in 517 BC. According to conflicting sources, King Jeconiah was born in either 615 or 605 BC, and taken prisoner by the Babylonians in 597 BC. According to the Jehoiachin's Rations Tablets, discovered by archeologists excavating ancient Babylon, Jeconiah had sons by 592 BC, meaning his heir Shealtiel had already been born. While it is not clear when Shealtiel's son Zerubbabel was born, as this was his oldest son, and he was at least nominally wealthy, his firstborn son was likely born before he turned 25, meaning

Zerubbabel would have been over 50 in Darius I's 5th regal year. If 1st Ezra is correct, that it was Zerubbabel's son Jehoiakim, he would have been much younger, likely under 30 in Darius I's second regal year.

However, in addition to the conflict within the text of the various Ezra and Nehemiah books, which claim that Artaxerxes stopped the rebuilding of Jerusalem before Darius restarted it, there is the fact that by Darius' second year, he was quickly becoming the strongest king that Persia ever had. Rebellions within Babylon and Egypt had been put down, and he was preparing to launch campaigns to expand the empire into Central Asia, and northern India. In 513 BC he launched an invasion of Europe, and marched his army through the Balkans and Ukraine, before building a series of forts along the Volga-Don portage. When he returned to Persia, the region of southern modern Ukraine was considered part of the Persian empire, a situation which continued for over 50 years. There simply was no reason to raze Jerusalem under his rule, nor any records of disorder in the region.

When the work stoppage of Artaxerxes is added to the timeline, with Artaxerxes I being Darius I's grandson who reigned between 465 and 424 BC, then the King Darius who restarted the work in Jerusalem has to have been Darius II, who ruled between 423 and 404 BC. This clearly means that the 'son of Shealtiel' was a male heir, and not the actual son of Shealtiel. This also explains why he was called the son of Pediah, which was another regal name, however, does not explain how the records got so confused. The confusion regarding whether it was Jehoiakim or Zerubbabel who traveled to Jerusalem with the High Priest Jesus / Joshuarebellion, appears to be the result of this Jehoiakim being excised from the records as a false messiah, which would have happened if he led the Judahites in a failed rebellion. As something caused Jerusalem to be razed shortly before Nehemiah arrived in 385 BC, and the Phoenicians were rebelling in 380 BC, it seems likely that whoever was leading Jerusalem was also rebelling.

2 Codex Vaticanus: Thermeleth (ⲑⲉⲣⲙⲉⲗⲉⲑ)

• Leningrad Codex in Ezra section of Ezra-Nehemiah: Tel Melach (תֵּל מֶלַח).

• Leningrad Codex in Nehemiah section of Ezra-Nehemiah: Tel Melach (תֵּל מָלַח)

3 Codex Vaticanus: Thelersas (ⲑⲉⲗⲉⲣⲥⲁⲥ)

• Leningrad Codex in Ezra and Nehemiah sections of Ezra-Nehemiah: Tel Charsha (תֵּל חַרְשָׁא)

4 Codex Vaticanus: Charaath (ⲭⲁⲣⲁⲁⲑ)

• Leningrad Codex in Ezra and Nehemiah sections of Ezra-Nehemiah: keruv (כְּרוּב)

The Masoretic version of Ezra (2ⁿᵈ Ezra) includes this name as a geographic term, not the name of a leader of the community. The Hebrew spelling of the name is the word meaning 'Cherub,' making it an unlikely name for a Babylonian town. If this was a geographic term, it could have been a reference to the Khabur River, or a settlement on it, where Ezekiel claimed to have seen Cherubs. This would explain why the Judahites in question could not trace their linage, as they would have been Samaritans that were relocated by the Assyrians.

5 Codex Vaticanus: Adan (ᴀᴅᴀɴ)

• Leningrad Codex in Ezra sections of Ezra-Nehemiah: addan (אַדָּן). Translation: base

• Leningrad Codex in Nehemiah sections of Ezra-Nehemiah: addon (אַדּוֹן). Translation: lord

This variation changes the Hebrew words from 'cherub base said,' to 'cherub lord said,' which then, when including the Greek words missing from the Masoretic Text, makes the phase mean 'following what the cherub lord said.' While this may be the original meaning of the now-lost Aramaic or Phoenician (Samaritan or Judahite) text of 1ˢᵗ Ezra, it is not what the Septuagint or Masoretic Text state any longer.

6 Codex Vaticanus: Amar (ᴀᴍᴀρ)

• Leningrad Codex in Ezra and Nehemiah sections of Ezra-Nehemiah: immer (אָמַר). Translation: said

7 Codex Vaticanus: Touban (ΤΟΥΒᴀΝ)

• Leningrad Codex in Ezra and Nehemiah sections of Ezra-Nehemiah: Toviyyah (טוֹבִיָּה).

This appears to be a reference to Tobian Judahites (Τουβιανοὺς Ιουδαίους) mentioned in 2ⁿᵈ Maccabees, who were likely followers of the author of the book of Tobit, which was set in Assyria and Media.

8 Codex Vaticanus: Ioddous (ιΟᴧᴧΟΥϹ)

• Leningrad Codex in Ezra and Nehemiah sections of Ezra-Nehemiah: varzillai (בַּרְזִלָּי). Translation: ferrous

The Masoretic texts does not use the name Ioddous, but instead son of Varzillai was married to the daughter of Varzillai. In 2ⁿᵈ Ezra and Masoretic Ezra it is clarified that he married the daughter of Varzillai, and took his name instead of keeping his own.

9 Codex Vaticanus: Aygian (ᴀΥΓιᴀΝ)

Aygian is not mentioned in the Masoretic text, which mention 'the daughters of Varzillai.'

10 Codex Vaticanus: Pharzellaeou (ΦΑΡΖΕΛΛΑΙΟΥ)

• Leningrad Codex in Ezra and Nehemiah sections of Ezra-Nehemiah: Varzillai (בַרְזִלָּי).

11 Codex Vaticanus: Neemias cae Attharias (νεεμιας και ατθαριας)

• Leningrad Codex in Ezra section of Ezra-Nehemiah: hattirshata (הַתִּרְשָׁתָא)

The term used in the Masoretic Text is interpreted as meaning something like 'governor,' however, it is not the Hebrew, Aramaic, Persian, or Babylonian word for governor. The Persian word for governor, xšaçapāvan (𒀯𒈦𒆪𒊑𒅖𒉌) is transliterated in the Hebrew version of Esther as achashdarpan (אֲחַשְׁדַּרְפָּן), which makes hattirshata (הַתִּרְשָׁתָא) an unlikely transliteration. The word that the author was likely trying to transliterate, was the Persian word artshtaran (ارتشتاران) which translates as military 'chieftain.' This would mean the 'artshtaran' was not Nehemiah, but the Persian military commander in Judea, which would explain why the Septuagint treats them as separate people. In the Masoretic Text, Nehemiah is specifically listed as being the 'military governor' in the later section when Ezra is present.

12 Codex Vaticanus: anastê archiereus endedymenos tên dêlôsin cae tên alêthian (ΑΝΑСΤΗΙ ΑΡΧΙΕΡΕΥС ΕΝΔΕΔΥΜΕΝΟС ΤΗΝ ΔΗΛΩСΙΝ ΚΑΙ ΤΗΝ ΑΛΗΘΕΙΑΝ).

Translation: the rising of a high-priest dressed who could explain and not lie.

• Leningrad Codex in Ezra section of Ezra-Nehemiah: amod kohen le'urim uletummim (עֲמֹד כֹּהֵן לְאוּרִים וּלְתֻמִּים). Translation: standing of the priest with the Urim and the Thummim

• Leningrad Codex in Nehemiah section of Ezra-Nehemiah: amod hakkohen le'urim vetummim (עֲמֹד הַכֹּהֵן לְאוּרִים וְתֻמִּים). Translation: standing of the priest with the Urim and Thummim

The Hebrew translations refer to the urim and thummim artifacts that are believed to have been used for cleromancy in the Torah. They were used by the high priests in the books of the Kingdoms (Masoretic Samuel and Kings), and attached to the high-priest's breastplate. The term may translate as 'lights and perfections,' however, this is not universally accepted.

13 Codex Vaticanus: Asbasareth (ΑϹΒΑϹΑΡΕΘ)

Esarhaddon is properly known as Asaraddon (Ασαραδδων) in Greek, however, this does appear to be a reference to Esarhaddon, as the identical story in 2ⁿᵈ Ezra refers to Esarhaddon. Esarhaddon is the more common name of King Aššur-Aha-Iddina, Sennacherib's youngest son and heir. The name Esarhaddon is derived from the Latin Hazor Haddan, which was in turn derived from the Greek Asarchaddon

(Ασαρχαδδων), which was used in direct translations from Assyrian texts. The term Asordan (Ασορδαν) used in the Septuagint appears to be a transliteration from a Hebrew text, however, not a Proto-Masorete text, as the name is quite different.

14 This final verse of chapter 5 is not in all copies of the Septuagint.

1st Ezra: Chapter 6

Now, in the second year of the reign of Darius, Haggai and Zachariah the son of Iddo, the prophets, prophesied to the Judahites in Judea and Jerusalem in the name of the Lord God in Israel, who was in them. Then Zerubbabel the son of Salatiel, and Jesus the son of Jehozadak, rose up and began to build the Temple of the Lord in Jerusalem, with the prophets of the Lord helping them. At the same time Tattannu[1] the governor of Syria and Phoenicia came to them, with Tishtrya-boznai[2] and his companions, and asked them, "By whose authority do you build this temple and this roof, and perform all the other things? Who are the workmen that perform these things?"

Nevertheless, the elders of the Judahites obtained favor because the Lord had visited the captivity. They were not stopped from building, until the time that authority was given to them by Darius, and an answer was received. The following is a copy of the letter which Governor Tattannu of Syria and Phoenicia, and Tishtrya-boznai, with their companions, rulers in Syria and Phoenicia, wrote and sent to Darius:

To King Darius,

Greetings,

Let all things be known to our Lord-of-Kings, that having traveled into the country of Judea, and entered into the city of Jerusalem, we found in the city of Jerusalem the elders of the Judahites that were of the captives building a temple to the Lord, great and new, of cut and costly stones, with timber already laid for the walls. Those works are done with great speed, and the work goes on prosperously in their hands, and with all glory and diligence is it made.

We asked these elders, 'By whose commandment do you build this temple, and lay the foundations of these works?' Intending that we might inform you in writing, we demanded of them who were the leaders, and we required of them the names in writing of their leading men.

They gave us this answer, 'We are the servants of the Lord which made the sky and earth. As for this temple, it was built many years ago by a king of Israel, great and strong, and was completed. But when our fathers provoked God to anger and sinned against the Lord of Israel, Shamayim[3] gave them over into the power of King Nebuchadnezzar of Babylon, of the Chaldeans, who tore down the temple and burned it, and took away the people as captives to Babylon. But in the first year that King Cyrus reigned over the land of Babylon, King Cyrus wrote to rebuild this temple. The holy vessels of gold and of silver, that Nebuchadnezzar had carried away out of the Temple in Jerusalem, and had set them in his own temple, those King Cyrus brought out again from the temple in Babylon, and they were delivered to Zerubbabel, and to Sheshbazzar the governor, with the commandment that he should take the vessels and place them in the temple in Jerusalem, and that the Temple of the Lord should be built in its place. Then the same Sheshbazzar came here and laid the foundations of the Temple of the Lord in Jerusalem, and from that time to this, it is still being built, and it is not yet finished.'

Now, therefore, if it seems good to the king, let a search be made among the records of King Cyrus. If it is found that the building of the Temple of the Lord in Jerusalem has been done with the consent of King Cyrus, and if our Lord-of-Kings agrees, let him let us know.

Then King Darius commanded to search among the records in Babylon, and also in the palace at Ecbatana[4] in the land of Media, where there was found a scroll in which these things were recorded. In the first year of the reign of King Cyrus, Cyrus commanded that the Temple of the Lord at Jerusalem should be rebuilt, where they will sacrifice with eternal fire.[5] Its height will be sixty cubits and the width sixty cubits, with three rows of cut stones, and one row of new wood of that country, and the expenses of it to be given out of the house of King Cyrus. The holy vessels of the Temple of the Lord, both of gold and silver, that Nebuchadnezzar took out of the house at Jerusalem, and brought to Babylon, should be restored to the house at Jerusalem, and be set in the place where they were before."

Therefore he commanded that Tattannu, the governor of Syria and Phoenicia, and Tishtrya-boznai, and their companions, and those which were appointed rulers in Syria and Phoenicia, should be careful not to interfere with the land, but allow Zerubbabel, the servant of the Lord and governor of Judea, and the elders of the Judahites, to build the Temple of the Lord in that place:

I have commanded also to have it rebuilt fully, and that they look diligently to help those that are from the captivity of the Judahites, until the Temple of the Lord is finished, out of the tribute of Coele-Syria and Phoenicia a portion is to be carefully given to these men for the sacrifices of the Lord, that is, to Governor Zerubbabel for bulls, rams, lambs, grain, salt, wine, and oil, and so on, annually without further question, as the priests that are in Jerusalem will require daily. Those offerings may be made to the Highest God[6] for the king and his children, and that they may pray for their lives. He commanded that whoever should transgress or make light of anything whether spoken or written, should be taken from his home and hung in a tree, and all his goods seized for the king. The Lord. therefore, whose name is there called on, destroys every king and nation, that stretched out his hand to stop or damage the Temple of the Lord in Jerusalem.

I, King Darius, have commanded that obeying these things be done with diligence.

1st Ezra: Chapter 6 Notes

1 Codex Vaticanus: Sisinnês (ϲιϲιΝΝΗϹ)

This is sometimes believed to be a reference to 'Tattenai, governor of Across-the-River,' the Satrap of Syria and Lebanon, who is recorded in cuneiform tablets dating to the year 502 BC, year 20 of Darius I's reign. Year 2 of Darius II was 421 BC, 81 years later, making this unlikely. Several cuneiform tablets bearing the name Tattenai have survived as part of what may have been a family archive, suggesting that the position of satrap in Syria and Lebanon may have been hereditary in the 5th century BC.

The name used in this translation is normalized as Tattenai based on the name in 2nd Ezra, the Masoretic version of Ezra, and the cuneiform tablets.

2 Codex Vaticanus: Sathrabouzanês (ϹΑΘΡΑΒΟΥΖΑΝΗϹ)

• Leningrad Codex in Ezra sections of Ezra-Nehemiah: Shetar bovznai (שְׁתַר בּוֹזְנַי)

The meaning of the name is debated, however, it is accepted as being Old Persian. Phonetically, the name translates as 'Tishtrya delivers,' in Old Persian. Tishtrya was a rain and fertility deity/being in the Avesta, the Zoroastrian holy book, as a result, the name Tishtrya-boznai is used in this translation.

3 Codex Vaticanus: ouranion (ΟΥΡΑΝΙΟΝ). Translation: skies

• Leningrad Codex in Ezra sections of Ezra-Nehemiah: le'elah shemayya (שְׁמַיָּא לֶאֱלָהּ). Translation: the god sky

The Greek translation is a variant spelling of ouraniôn (ουράνιων), which is the plural form of 'sky' or 'Uranus' (the Greek sky-god). In other sections of the Masoretic Text, the term Shamayim (שָׁמַיִם) was used, however, the use of shemayya (שְׁמַיָּא), instead of the Hebrew term shamayim, reflects the Aramaic source text that would have used the term šmayya (ܫܡܝܐ). The Aramaic shmayya, Hebrew shamayim, Canaanite šmm (𐤔𐤌𐤌), and Ugaritic šmm (𐎌𐎎𐎎), all represent various spellings of both the term 'skies,' and the name of the 'sky-god.' The worship of the armies of Shamayim was banned by King Josiah in Judah circa 625 BC. In 1st Ezra, the term appears to have been used as part of the larger 'sky-god' religion of the era, and not a reference to Shamayim per se. The major sky-god of the era was the Zoroastrian Ahura Mazda, however, the Arameans did continue to worship Shamayim as Baalshamin (ܒܥܠ ܫܡܝܢ) in Palmyra.

The archaeological evidence from the Israelite colony in southern Egypt supports the god Yhw as being viewed as the sky-god by the Persian Era. While he was still married to Anat at the beginning of the Persian era, it appears he had become a monotheist god, like Ahura Mazda, by the beginning of the Greek era. It is unclear if the Persian and Babylonian Judahites and Benjaminites that returned to Judea used the name, or simply called him by the title Bel, Babylonian for 'Lord,' however, there are no surviving copies of 1st Ezra with the name Iaw (Ιαω), the Greek spelling of Yhw, in them, and there is no surviving Aramaic of Hebrew translation with the name in those languages either.

4 Codex Vaticanus: Ekbatánois (ЄКВАТΑΝΟΙC)

Ecbatana was the Greek translation of Hangmatāna (𒀔𒀔𒐊-𒈨𒄷𒅎𒀹), the capital of the earlier Median Empire and the summer capital of the Persian Empire. Its name translates in Median as 'the place of gathering.' The location of the city has been debated, and it may have been moved during the Median Empire. By the Persian era it was a city, however, the city the Greeks described has not been firmly identified.

5 Codex Vaticanus: opou epithyousin dia pyros endelechous (ΟΠΟΥ ЄΠΙΘΥΟΥϹΙΝ ΔΙΑ ΠΥΡΟϹ ЄΝΔЄΛЄΧΟΥϹ). Translation: where sacrifice upon by fire (or wheat) continuous (or eternal)

Eternal Fire is not an ancient Israelite commandment from the Torah, however is a Zoroastrian requirement, which caused the Muslims to later called them fire-worshipers. It is clear from this scroll that King Cyrus believed it was a Zoroastrian temple being built in Jerusalem.

6 Codex Vaticanus: theô tô hypsistô (ϴЄѠТѠΥϯΙϹΤѠ). Translation: god the highest

• Leningrad Codex in Ezra section of Ezra-Nehemiah: le'elah shemayya (שְׁמַיָּא לֶאֱלָהּ). Translation: the god (on Aramaic, or goddess in Hebrew) sky (or Shamayim)

The Hebrew translation is clearly based on an Aramaic source text, as both words are Aramaic. The term elah (𐤀𐤋𐤄 / אֱלָהּ), translates 'goddess' in Hebrew, and as 'god' in Aramaic, while shemayya / šmayya (𐤔𐤌𐤉𐤀 / שְׁמַיָּא) is not proper Hebrew, but the Aramaic word meaning 'skies,' and the name of the god the Hebrews called Shamayim.

As both the Greek and Hebrew translations must have been translated from an Aramaic source, this variant indicates that there were at least two variants of the Aramaic book of Ezra before the translations were made. It also indicates a high probability that the title 'Highest God' referred to Shamayim in the Persian Era. However, it should be noted that Darius was a Zoroastrian, and almost certainly would have been referring to Ahura Mazda as the Highest God. It is possible that the variation found in the Masoretic Text, which names Shemaiyo, was an attempt by a scribe to clarify which 'highest god' the letter was about. If so, the edit likely took place in the Greek era, after the Persian Ahura Mazda was no longer the supreme god, and the sky-god Zeus was. In any event, this edit had to have been done in Aramaic, before the book of Ezra was translated into Samaritan, Judahite, or Hebrew.

1st Ezra: Chapter 7

Then Tattannu the governor of Coele-Syria and Phoenicia, and Tishtrya-boznai, with their companions following the commandments of King Darius, did very carefully oversee the holy works, assisting the elders of the Judahites and leaders of the temple. The holy works prospered, as Haggai and Zachariah the prophets prophesied. They finished these things by the commandment of the Lord God in Israel, and with the consent of Cyrus, Darius, and Artaxerxes, the kings of Persia. And so was the holy temple finished on the 23rd day of the month Adar,[1] in the sixth year of King Darius of the Persians. The Israelites, the priests, and the Levites, and others that were of the captives, that were added to them, following the ordinance written in the book of Moses.

At the dedication of the Temple of the Lord, they offered 100 bulls, 200 rams, and 400 lambs, and 12 goats for the sin of all Israel, according to the number of the chief of the tribes of Israel. The priests, and also the Levites, stood arrayed in their vestments, according to their families, in the service of the Lord God in Israel, following the book of Moses, with the porters at every gate. The Israelites who were from the captives held the Passover on the fourteenth day of the first month, and after that, the priests and the Levites were sanctified.

They who were of the captives were not all sanctified together, but the Levites were all sanctified together. So they offered the Passover for all of those of the captives and their brothers the priests, and for themselves. The Israelites that returned from the captives ate, and all those who had separated themselves from the abominations of the people of the land and served the Lord. They kept the feast of unleavened bread seven days, celebrating before the Lord, as he had turned the counsel of the king of Assyria² towards them, to strengthen their hands in the works of the Lord God of Israel.

1st Ezra: Chapter 7 Notes

1 Codex Vaticanus: adar (ⲁⲇⲁⲣ)

• Leningrad Codex in Ezra sections of Ezra-Nehemiah: Adar (אֲדָר)

Adar is the twelfth month in the Hebrew calendar. The Hebrew Calendar is lunisolar, and so the months move somewhat in comparison to the Gregorian Calendar, and therefore the equivalent could be anywhere between February and April, depending on the year. However, Adar falls before the northern winter solstice, and therefore generally falls in March on the Gregorian calendar.

2 Codex Vaticanus: basileôs Assyriôn (ⲃⲁⲥⲓⲗⲉⲱⲥ ⲁⲥⲥⲩⲣⲓⲱⲛ). Translation: king of Assyrians

• Leningrad Codex in Ezra sections of Ezra-Nehemiah: melech-ashur (מֶלֶךְ־אַשּׁוּר). Translation: king of Assur

The reference to the King of Assyria seems to indicate that there were many Samaritans in the returning Israelites, as the Assyrians had conquered Samaria, not Judah. By the time that Judah was destroyed by the Neo-Babylonian Empire, Babylon had already conquered Assyria.

1st Ezra: Chapter 8

After these things, when Artaxerxes the king of the Persians reigned, came Ezra the son of Seraiah, the son of Uzziah, the son of Hilkiah, the son of Shallum, the son of Zadok, the son of Ahitub, the son of Omri, the son of Uzziah, the son of Meraioth, the son of Zerahiah, the son of Uzzi, the son of Bukki, the son of Abishua, the son of Phinehas, the son of Eleazar, the son of Aaron the first priest. This Ezra traveled from Babylon, as a scribe, being well trained in the law of Moses, that was given by the God in Israel.

The king honored him, as he found grace in his sight in all his requests. Traveling with him to Jerusalem were also certain Israelites, from among the priest of the Levites, and the holy singers, porters, and ministers of the temple. In the seventh year of the reign of Artaxerxes, in the fifth month, this was the king's seventh year, they traveled from Babylon in the first day of the first month, and came to Jerusalem, on a prosperous journey, which the Lord gave them. Ezra had very great skill, and he omitted nothing of the law and commandments of the Lord, but taught all Israel the ordinances and judgments. The copy of the commission, which was written by King Artaxerxes, came with Ezra the cohen,[1] and scribe of the law of the Lord follows:

"King Artaxerxes to Ezra the priest and scribe of the law of the Lord, greeting,

Having decided to deal graciously, I have given an order, that some of the nation of the Judeans, and of the priests and Levites being within our realm, as are willing and desiring, should go with you to Jerusalem. As many as want to, let them leave with you, as it seems good both to me and my seven friends, the counselors. That who may look to the affairs of Judea and Jerusalem, agreeably to that which is in the law of the Lord, and carry the gifts to the Lord of Israel to Jerusalem, which I and my friends have vowed, and all the gold and silver that can be found in the country of Babylon, to the Lord in Jerusalem, with that which is given also from the people for the Temple of the Lord God at Jerusalem, and so silver and gold may be collected for bulls, rams, and lambs, and things to do with it, to the goal that they may offer sacrifices to the Lord on the altar of the Lord God, that is in Jerusalem.

Whatever you and your brothers will do with the silver and gold, do it according to the will of your god. The holy vessels of the Lord, which are given you for the use of the temple of your god, which is in Jerusalem, you will set before your god in Jerusalem. Whatever else you will remember for the use of the Temple of God, you will give it out of the king's treasury.

I, King Artaxerxes, have also commanded the keepers of the treasures in Syria and Phoenicia, that whatever Ezra the priest and the scribe of the law of the highest god will send for, they should give it to him quickly, up to a maximum of one hundred talents of silver, likewise also of wheat up to a hundred cors, and a hundred vats of wine, and other things in abundance. Let all things be done according to the law of God, diligently, to the highest god, that anger does not come against the kingdom of the king and his sons. I command you also, that you require no tax, nor any other imposition, of any of the priests, or Levites, or holy singers, or porters, or ministers of the temple, or any that work in this temple, and that no man has authority to impose anything on them.

You, Ezra, according to the wisdom of God ordain judges and justices, that they may judge in all Syria and Phoenicia all those that know the law of your god, and those that do not know it you will teach. Whoever will transgress the law of your god, the king will punish diligently, whether it is by death, or other punishment, by penalty of money, or by imprisonment."

Then Ezra the scribe said, "Blessed be the only Lord God of my fathers, who has put these things into the heart of the king, to glorify his house that is in Jerusalem. He has honored me in the sight of the king, and his counselors, and all his friends and nobles. Therefore, I was encouraged by the help of the Lord God and gathered together men of Israel to go up with me.

These are the chiefs according to their families and several dignities, that returned with me from Babylon in the reign of King Artaxerxes:

Of the sons of Phinehas, was Gershom.

Of the sons of Ithamar, was Daniel.

Of the sons of David, was Hattush the son of Shekaniah.

Of the sons of Pharez, was Zachariah, and with him were 150 men.

Of the sons of Pahathmoab, was Elihoenai the son of Zerahiah, and with him were 200 men.

Of the sons of Zathoe, was Shekaniah the son of Jehiel, and with him were 300 men.

Of the sons of Adin, was Ebed the son of Jonathan, and with him were 250 men.

Of the sons of Elam, was Josiah son of Athaliah, and with him were 70 men.

Of the sons of Shephatiah, was Zerahiah son of Michael, and with him were 70 men.

Of the sons of Joab, was Obadiah son of Jehiel, and with him were 212 men

Of the sons of Banid, was Assalimoth son of Josiphiah, and with him were 160 men.

Of the sons of Bebai, was Zachariah son of Bebai, and with him were 28 men.

Of the sons of Astath, was Johanan son of Hakkatan, and with him were 110 men.

Of the sons of Adonikam the last; these are the names of them: Eliphelet, Jeiel, and Shemaiah, and with them were 70 men.

Of the sons of Bigvai, was Uthai the son of Istalcurus, and with him were 70 men.

These I gathered together at the river called Theras, where we pitched our tents for three days, and then I surveyed them. When I had found none of the priests and Levites, then I sent word to Eleazar, and Iduel, and Masman, Elnathan, Mamaias, Jarib, Nathan, Eunatan, Zachariah, and Meshullam, principal men and learned. I commanded them that they should go to Iddo the captain, who was in the place of the treasury, and commanded them that they should speak to Iddo, and his brothers, and to the treasurers in that place, to send us such men as might execute the priests' office in the Temple of the Lord.

By the mighty hand of the Lord, they brought to us skillful men of the sons of Mahli the son of Levi, the son of Israel: Hashabiah, and his sons, and his brothers, who were eighteen. Hashabiah, Annuus, Osaias his brother, of the sons of Channuneus, and their sons, were twenty men. Of the servants of the temple that David had ordained, and the principal men for the service of the Levites, the servants of the temple were two hundred and twenty, the list of whose names were showed.

There, I vowed a fast to the young men before the Lord, to the desire from him of a prosperous journey both for us and them that were with us, for our children, and the livestock, as I was ashamed to ask from the king infantry and cavalry to safeguard us against our adversaries. For, we had said to the king, that the power of our Lord God should be with them that seek him, to support them in all ways. Again, we implored the Lord regarding these things and found him favorable to us. Then I separated twelve of the chief of the priests, Sherebiah, Assanias, and ten men of their brothers with them. I weighed them the gold, and the silver, and the holy vessels of the Temple of the Lord, which the king, and his council, and the princes, and all Israel, had given. When I had weighed it, I delivered to them six hundred and fifty talents of silver, and silver vessels of a hundred talents, and a hundred talents of gold, twenty golden vessels, and twelve vessels of brass, even of fine brass, glittering like gold.

I said to them, "Both you are holy to the Lord, and the vessels are holy, and the gold and the silver is vowed to the Lord, the god of our fathers. You guard them, and keep them until you deliver them to the chief of the

priests and Levites, and the principal men of the families
of Israel, in Jerusalem, into the chambers of the Temple
of God. "

So the priests and the Levites, who had received the
silver and the gold and the vessels, brought them to
Jerusalem, into the Temple of the Lord. From the river
Theras, we departed the twelfth day of the first month
and came to Jerusalem by the mighty hand of the Lord,
which was with us, and from the beginning of our journey the Lord delivered us from every enemy, and so
we came to Jerusalem. When we had been there three
days, the gold and silver that was weighed were delivered in the Temple of the Lord on the fourth day, to
Meremoth the priest, the son of Uriah. With him was
Eleazar the son of Phinehas, and with them were Jozabad the son of Jesus, and Moeth the son of Sabban,
Levites.

All were delivered to them by count and weight. All
the weight of them was written down that hour. Moreover, they that had come out of the captivity offered sacrifice to the Lord God of Israel, including 12 bulls for all
Israel, and 96 rams, 72 lambs, and 12 goats for a peace offering. All of them a sacrifice to the Lord.

They delivered the king's commandments to the
king's stewards and the governors of Coele-Syria and

Phoenicia, and they honored the people and the Temple of God. Now when these things were done, the rulers came to me, and said, "The nation of Israel, the princes, the priests, and Levites, have not sent away from them the foreign people in the land, or the pollution of the Canaanites, Greeks,[2] Perizzites, Jebusites, Moabites, Egyptians, and Edomites. Both they, and their sons, have married their daughters, and the holy seed is mixed with the foreign people of the land, and from the beginning of this matter the rulers and the great men have been partakers of this iniquity."

As soon as I had heard these things, I tore my clothes, and the holy garment, and shaved off the hair from my head, and my beard, and sat down sad and very heavy. So all those who were then moved at the word of the Lord God of Israel assembled to me, while I mourned for the iniquity, but I sat still, full of heaviness until the evening sacrifice.

Then, rising from the fast, with my clothes and the holy garment torn, and bowing my knees, and stretching out my hands to the Lord, I said, "Lord, I am confused and ashamed before your face. For our sins are multiplied above our heads, and our ignorance has reached up to the sky. Since the time of our fathers we have been, and are still in great sin, even to today. For our sins and our fathers', we with our brothers and our kings and our priests were given up to the kings of the earth, to the sword, and captivity, and as a plunder in shame, until today. Now, some measure of mercy has been showed to us from you, Lord, that there should be left us a root and a name in the place of your sanctuary, for us to discover a light in the Temple of the Lord God, and to give us food in the time of our servitude. Yes, when we were in slavery, we were not forgotten by the Lord, but he made us gracious before the kings of Persia so that they gave us food. Yes, and honored the Temple of the Lord, and raised the desolate Zion, that they have given us a save dwelling in Judea and Jerusalem. Now, Lord, what will we say, having these things? For we have transgressed your commandments, which you gave by the hand of your servants the prophets, saying, 'The land which you enter into to possess as a heritage, is a land polluted with the pollution of the foreigners in the land, and they have filled it with their uncleanness. Therefore, you will not join your daughters to their sons, neither will you take their daughters to your sons. Moreover, you will never seek to have peace with them, so you may be strong, and eat the good things of the land, and that you may leave the inheritance of the land to your children forever.' All that has happened, is done to us for our wicked works and great sins, for you, Lord, did make our sins light, did give to us such a root, but we have turned back again to

transgress your law and mingled ourselves with the uncleanness of the nations of the land. Might you not be angry with us and destroy us, until you had left us neither
root nor seed or name? Lord of Israel, you are true, for
we have left a root this day. Look, now we are before
you in our iniquities, for we can't stand any longer because of these things before you."

As Ezra, in his prayer made his confession, weeping,
and lying flat on the ground before the temple, a very
great crowd of men and women and children gathered
around him from Jerusalem, for there was great weeping among the crowd. Then Shechaniah the son of Jehiel, one of the sons of Israel, called out, and said, "Ezra,
we have sinned against the Lord God! We have married
foreign women of the nations of the land, and now is all
Israel lost. Let us make an oath to the Lord, that we will
divorce all our wives, which we have taken of the hea-
then, and their children, like as you have decreed, and as
many as do obey the law of the Lord. Rise and put in ex-
ecution, for to you does this matter appertain, and we
will be with you! Do valiantly!"

So Ezra arose and took an oath of the chief of the
priests and Levites of all Israel to do these things, and so
they swore.

1st Ezra: Chapter 8 Notes

1 Codex Vaticanus: ierea (ιερεא). Translation: priest, diviner, holy one

- Leningrad Codex in Ezra sections of Ezra-Nehemiah: chahana (כָּהֲנָא)

Cohens are a division of the Levites that can trace their lineage back to Aaron, the first priest of Israel.

2 Codex Vaticanus: Chettaeôn (χεττλιωn)

- Leningrad Codex in Ezra (2nd Ezra): Chitti (חִתִּי).

Translation: Cypriots (or Greeks)

This term has created a great deal of confusion since the misidentification of the ruins of the Neshites as being 'Hittite' in the 1800s. The modern archaeological name 'Hittite,' is not derived from an ancient name for the culture applied by themselves, or anyone else, but rather adopted from the biblical reference to a then-unknown civilization somewhere in the region. There was an ancient culture in the region called the Hattians, however, they were conquered by the Nesites before 1700 BC, and subsequently disappeared from the historic records.

The name was applied to culture today referred to as 'Hittites,' before the 'Hittite' language had been translated, and is incorrect. Since 1906, excavations at Boğazköy, the ancient 'Hittite' capital Hattusa have uncovered more than 10,000 'Hittite' texts, including the royal achieve. The actual name of the 'Hittite' language and people was Nešili (𒉌𒅆𒇷), which is now rendered in some academic literate as Nesite or Neshite. As early as the mid-1800s some scholars disputed the identification of the Nesites as the Biblical Hittites, including the Orientalist Max Müller, who was one of many claiming the Biblical Hittites were ancient Greeks or some other Mediterranean people. Later in the Septuagint's translation of the Maccabees, the similar term Chettiim (Χεττιιμ) as a reference to all Greek-speaking lands.

In the 1st century AD, the Jewish historian Josephus reported that Cethima was the name of Cyrus in Aramaic, and the Chettim were the descendants of Noah's grandson Chethimus, who had settled on Cyprus. Josephus reported that the name was preserved in the Greek name of the town Cition (Κίτιον). Most historians view it as more likely that the Aramaic name was derived from the city-state of Cition, which was known as Kåtjåy (𓈖𓏏𓇋𓍿𓀭) in Egyptian records from the New Kingdom Era in the late Bronze Age, and Kt (𐤊𐤕) or Kty (𐤊𐤕𐤉) in Phoenician records from the early Iron Age. While this may be the origin of the term, by the era of the Neo-Assyrian era, the term must have also referred to other Greek islands, as both the prophets Isaiah and Ezekiel used the term 'Islands of Kittim.' As the term referred to all Greek lands in Aramaic by the time of Ezekiel, the translations of 'Greece' and 'Greeks' are used here.

1st Ezra: Chapter 9

Ezra rose from the court in the temple and went to the chamber of Johanan the son of Elijahib, and remained there, and ate no meat nor drank any water, mourning for the great sins of the multitude. There was a proclamation in all Judea and Jerusalem to all those that were of the captives, that they should be gathered together in Jerusalem, that whoever did not meet there in two or three days as the ruling elders had ordered, their livestock should be seized for the use of the temple, and he himself expelled from among those that were captives.

In three days, all those of the tribes of Judah and Benjamin were gathered together in Jerusalem, on the twentieth day of the ninth month. All the multitude sat shivering in the broad court of the temple because of the terrible weather. Ezra got up, and shouted to them, "You have transgressed the law in marrying foreign wives, and thereby increase the sins of Israel! Now by confessing give glory to the Lord God of our fathers! Do his will, and separate yourselves from the ethnic groups of this land, and the foreign women!"

Then the whole multitude cried, and said with a loud voice, "As you have spoken, we will do. But as the people are many, and it is terrible weather, we can't stand outside, and this is not a work of a day or two, seeing our sin in these things is spread far. Therefore, let the rulers of the multitude stay, and let all those of our lands that have foreign wives come at a time appointed, with the rulers and judges of every place, until we turn away the anger of the Lord from us for this matter."

Then Jonathan the son of Asahel, and Jahaziah the son of Tikvah took on this matter, and Meshullam and Shabbethai the Levites helped them. They that were of the captives did according to all these things. Ezra the priest called to him the principal men of their families, all by name, and on the first day of the tenth month, they sat together to examine the matter. So their cause that held foreign wives was brought to an end on the first day of the first month. Of the priests that had come together, and had foreign wives, there were found:

Of the sons of Jesus the son of Jehozadak, and his brothers: Maaseiah, Eleazar, Jarib, and Joadanus. They signed their names to divorced their wives and to offer rams to make reconciliation for their sins.

Of the sons of Immer: Hananiah, Zebadiah, Eanes, Shemaiah, and Jehiel, and Uzziah.

Of the sons of Pashur: Elioenai, Maaseiah, Ishmael, Nethanel, and Ocidelus and Talsas.

Of the Levites: Jehozabad, Shimei, Kelaiah who was called Kelita, Pethahiah, Judas, and Jonah.

Of the holy singers: Eliashib and Bacchurus.

Of the porters: Shallum and Telem.

Of those of Israel from the sons of Pharez: Hiermas, Eddias, Malchiah, Maelus, Eleazar, Asibias, and Benaiah.

Of the sons of Elam: Mattaniah, Zachariah, Jehiel, Jeremoth, and Aedias.

Of the sons of Zamoth: Eliadas, Elisimus, Othonias, Jarimoth, and Sabatus, and Sardeus.

Of the sons of Bebai: Johanan, and Hananiah and Jozabad, and Amatheis.

Of the sons of Mani: Olamus, Mamuchus, Jedeus, Jashub, Jasael, and Jeremoth.

Of the sons of Eri: Naathus, Moosias, Lacunus, Naidus, Mathanias, Sesthel, Balnuus, and Manasseas.

Of the sons of Sanaas: Elioenai, Aseas, Malchiah, Sabbeus, and Simon Chosameus.

Of the sons of Hushim: Altaneus, Matthias, Baanaia, Eliphelet, Manasseh, and Shimei.

Of the sons of Maani: Jeremiah, Momdis, Omaerus, Juel, Mabdai, Pelias, Anos, Carabasion, Enasibus, Mamnitanaimus, Elijahis, Bannus, Eliali, Samis, Shelemiah, and Nethaniah.

Of the sons of Ozora: Sesis, Esril, Azaelus, Samatus, Zambis, and Josephus.

Of the sons of Ethma: Mazitias, Zabadaias, Edes, Juel, Benaiah.

All these had taken foreign wives, and they divorced them and abandoned their children. The priests and Levites, and those who were of Israel lived in Jerusalem, and in the country, on the first day of the seventh month, so the Israelites returned to their homes.

The whole multitude came together with one accord into the broad place of the holy porch towards the east. They spoke to Ezra the priest and scribe, that he would bring the law of Moses, that was given of the Lord God of Israel. So Ezra the chief priest brought the law to the whole multitude of men and women, and to all the priests, to hear law on the first day of the seventh month. He read in the broad court before the holy porch from morning to midday, before both men and women, and the multitude gave heed to the law. Ezra the priest and scribe of the law stood at a pulpit of wood, which was made for that purpose.

There stood alongside him Mattathias, Shammua, Hananiah, Uzziah, Uriah, Ezecias, Balasamus, on the right hand. On his left hand stood Phaldaius, Mishael, Malchiah, Lothasubus, and Nabarias. Then Ezra took the book of the law before the crowd, for he sat honorably in the first place in the sight of them all. When he opened the law, they all immediately stood up. So Ezra blessed the Lord God, Highest God, Sabaoth Shaddai.[1] All the people replied, "Amen!" and lifting up their hands they fell to the ground and worshiped the Lord. Also, Jesus, Anus, Sarabias, Adinus, Jacubus, Sabateas, Auteas, Maianeas, and Kelita, Uzziah, and Joazabdus, and Hananiah, Biatas, the Levites, taught the law of the Lord, making them easy to understand.

Then Attharates spoke to Ezra the chief priest and reader, and to the Levites that taught the multitude saying, "Today is holy to the Lord! (They all wept when they heard the law.) Go then, and eat the fat, and drink the sweet, and send the part to them that have nothing. For this day is holy to the Lord! Do not be sad, for the Lord will bring you honor."

So the Levites published all things to the people, saying, "This day is holy to the Lord! Do not be sad."

Then they went their way, every one to eat and drink, and celebrate, and to share with those who had nothing, and to make great cheer. Because they understood the words in which they were instructed, and for which they had been assembled.

1ˢᵗ Ezra: Chapter 9 Notes

1 Codex Vaticanus: cyriô theô hypsistô theô sabaôth pantocratori (ⲕⲨⲢⲓⲱ ⲐⲈⲱ ⲨⲨⲓⲤⲦⲱ ⲐⲈⲱ ⲤⲀⲂⲀⲱⲐ ⲦⲧⲀⲚⲦⲟⲔⲢⲀⲦⲟⲢⲓ). Translation: lord god highest god Sabaoth omnipotent (or almighty)

• Leningrad Codex in Nehemiah section of Ezra: Yehvah ha'elohim haggadovl (יְהוָה הָאֱלֹהִים הַגָּדוֹל). Translation: Yehvah the god (in Neo-Babylonian, or gods in Aramaic, or goddesses in Hebrew) the great

The Greek and Hebrew translations clearly differ at this point, as the Greek translation includes twice as many terms. Both Ezra and Nehemiah would have written in an Aramaic dialect influenced by Persian and Neo-Babylonian, suggesting that the Hebrew translators simplified the verse. The pairing of Sabaoth (Σαβαωθ) and pantocratôri (παντοκράτορι), indicates that the Aramaic verse read 'Lord of the Elohim, highest god, Saboath Shaddai' as pantocratôr (παντοκράτωρ) was used as the translation of Šdy (שׁדי) in the older sections of the Tanakh, including Job, where the terms are mirrored between the Septuagint and Masoretic text 33 times. The Septuagint and Masoretic translations often differ in regards to the name or title Šdy, suggesting that the Aramaic and Canaanite (Judahite or Samaritan) source texts they worked from differed in regards to this word. The term was omitted throughout Cosmic Genesis, suggesting that when the word was first encountered the Greeks did not know how to interpret it, as Cosmic Genesis / Bereshít is the first book of the Torah, the first collection of Israelite texts probably translated at the Library of Alexandria.

It is equally possible that it was the earlier Aramaic translator who had omitted it, however, it was almost certainly in the Canaanite version the translator worked from, as it is used consistently in Bereshít, and is mentioned again when Moses god's name Ān is introduced in the Septuagint's Exodus.

The cause of the confusion over the term šdy, is likely due to the difference between the meaning of the word in Canaanite versus Aramaic. In Akkadian cuneiform, which was adopted as the written script by many cultures, the term was ᵈᵉⁱᵗʸšēdu (✳️𐎕), however, it referred to a 'protective spirit' or 'lesser god.' In the later Aramaic language, the word became šydå (𐎐𐎛𐎅𐎜), meaning 'demon' in the classical sense, as a type of muse or nymph. Whereas in Canaanite, šdy (𐎇𐎀𐎅) took on different meaning, generally interpreted as 'powerful' by the Early Classical Era, which is likely where the Greeks ultimately derived the term 'omnipotent' (παντοκράτορος), which was used later in the Septuagint where the Masoretic Text generally uses the term šdy.

This alternate interpretation of the šdy (𐎇𐎀𐎅) in Canaanite is likely due to the Egyptian New Kingdom era rule over Canaan, when Shed (𓊰𓏏𓃀𓈖, transliteration: šd), was worshiped in the region. Shed, who was often referred to as 'the savior,' was virtually identical to the earlier Canaanite god Resheph who was largely suppressed after the fall of the Hyksos dynasty.

In the Masoretic Book of Job, Eliphaz referred to humanity as the 'sons of Resheph' (בני-רשף) instead of the 'sons of

Adam,' and then uses šdy as the name of a god. This god šdy was explicitly listed alongside the god El in Masoretic Job, whereas in the Septuagint's Job they are not explicitly listed as two separate gods. The Greek translation of Šdy (שדי) in Job is consistent with most of the Septuagint, using a term that translates as 'omnipotent' (παντοκράτορος), however, the name El (אל) is generally translated as a word meaning 'strong' (ἰσχυρὸς). It is likely because the Masoretic Text lists them side by side, as 'god El and god Šdy,' (אל-אל ואל-שדי), which the Greek translators did not do, instead routinely dropping the second reference to a god when they were listed together.

The terms 'god Šdy' (אל-שדי) and 'god El' (אל-אל) are repeatedly found in the Masoretic version of Job, and are themselves direct translations of the same terms in Akkadian Cuneiform: deityšēdu (𒀭𒆘) and deityAn (𒀭𒀭). Unfortunately, the Akkadian meaning of the word šēdu was 'demonic,' which is likely the cause of it's redaction. Based on the linguistics of Masoretic Job, the text book existed in a hieratic Canaanite form during the Hyksos Dynasty, and therefore the name Resheph is not out of place, as Resheph was one of the main gods of the Hyksos rulers.

During the subsequent New Kingdom era, Resheph worship was suppressed due to his association with the earlier Hyksos dynasty. During the early New Kingdom era, holy texts about Resheph would have been updated to Shed (𓄞𓂧𓀭), which would have been transliterated into Canaanite using the Akkadian Cuneiform script in the late

New Kingdom era as ^{deity}šēdu (✱⊏⊟), before being translated into Canaanite using the Phoenician script in the early iron age as šdy (ᘔᐱꟿ), resulting in the confusing 'demonic' (ᑍᕦᐱᏉ) god in Aramaic. During the Neo-Babylonian era, after Judah had been occupied by Babylonia, the books of the Kingdoms (Masoretic Samuel and Kings) appear to have been compiled in cuneiform, from the older Phoenician script Chronicles of Samaria and Judah. During this translation, Sebittu (𒀭𒄿𒐊𒐊) appears to have been used as a translation for Shaddai, as ^{deity}šēdu (✱⊏⊟) had come to mean 'protective griffin,' during the Neo-Assyrian era. The Assyrian version of the word was Sebitti (𒐊𒀭𒐊), the god of war, which was associated with the Phrygian god Sabazdiôs (ꟙA8AꟊXOꟙ), which was later reinterpreted as Sabazios (Σαβάζιος) in the Greco-Roman era, who was viewed as the Phrygian version of Sabaoth. The Babylonian term Sebittu did not refer to a war god, but 'cosmic authority' during the Neo-Babylonian era. In the Old Akkadian language, the Sebittu (𒀭𒐊𒐊𒐊) had been the seven gods (sun, moon, and five planets) that ruled the sky, however, this usage had disappeared by the late bronze age, leaving only the vague concept of cosmic authority by the Neo-Babylonian era.

In this verse, the author appears to have used Shaddai as an epithet of Sabaoth, indicating he did not understand that one word was a translation of the other, explaining why the Hebrew translators simplified the verse.

2nd Ezra: Chapter 1

In the first year of King Cyrus[1] of the Persians, the words of the Lord[2] spoken by Jeremiah would come to pass, the Lord stirred up the spirit of King Cyrus of the Persians, and he issued a proclamation through all his kingdom in writing, saying,

King Cyrus of the Persians states,

"The Lord God of the sky[3] has given me all the kingdoms of the earth, and he has given me an order to build him a temple in Jerusalem, in Judea. Who are there among you of all his people? As his God will be with him, he will go to Jerusalem which is in Judea, and let him build the Temple of God of Israel; the God in Jerusalem. Let every one that is left leave from wherever he travels, and the men of his place will help him with silver, and gold, and goods, and livestock, together with the voluntary offering for the Temple of God that is in Jerusalem."

The chiefs of the families of Judah and Benjamin rose along with the priests, and the Levites, all who God aroused the spirit of, went to build the Temple of the Lord in Jerusalem. All that were around them strengthened their hands with vessels of silver and gold, and goods and livestock, and with presents, besides the voluntary offerings. King Cyrus brought out the vessels of the Temple of the Lord, which Nebuchadnezzar[4] had brought from Jerusalem, and put in the temple of his god. King Cyrus of the Persians brought them out by the hand of Mithradates[5] the treasurer, and he counted them for Sheshbazzar, the prince of Judah.[6] This was their number: thirty gold basins, and a thousand silver basins, twenty-nine changes, thirty golden goblets, and four hundred and ten double silver vessels, and a thousand other vessels. All the gold and silver vessels were five thousand and four hundred, including all that went up with Sheshbazzar from the place of transportation, from Babylon to Jerusalem.

2nd Ezra: Chapter 1 Notes

1 Codex Vaticanus: Kyrou (ΚΥΡΟΥ)

* Aleppo Codex: Kwrš (כורש)

* Leningrad Codex: Choresh (כּוֹרֶשׁ)

Kuruš (𒆪𒊏𒀸), more commonly called Cyrus II or Cyrus the Great today, established the Achaemenid Dynasty, and the first Persian Empire. Between 559 and 530 he conquered an empire that included most of modern Iran, Iraq, and Turkey. Cyrus II is generally accepted as being a Zoroastrian, as he ordered that an empty chariot be driving into battle alongside his own for Ahura Mazda to ride in. He is believed to have also been the king that ordered the construction of the Avestan archives, and the writing down of the Avestan literature, which had previously only been sung or chanted, however, Alexander III's destruction of the archives may make it impossible to know who ordered its construction.

2 Codex Vaticanus: cyriou (ΚΥΡΙΟΥ). Translation: ruler (or governor, main, major, primary, master, lord)

* Aleppo Codex: Yhwh (יהוה)

* Leningrad Codex: Yehvah (יְהוָה)

There are no early surviving copies of the Septuagint's version of Ezra which have the name Iaw (Ιαω) in it, like some of the other books of the Septuagint, and therefore it cannot be known conclusively if the name was ever in the Septuagint's Ezra or not. Nevertheless, Ezra, and Nehemiah, both use terminology that implies they were worshiping the Zoroastrian God Ahura Mazda, making the presence of the name unlikely in the original Greek translation, or the Aramaic source-text they translated from.

3 Codex Vaticanus: cyrios ho theos tou ouranou (ΚΥΡΙΟϹΟ ΘΕΟϹ ΤΟΥ ΟΥΡΑΝΟΥ). Translation: lord the god the Uranus (or the vaulted sky)

• Aleppo Codex: Yhwh ålhy hšmym (יהוה אלהי השמים). Translation: Yhwh goddess (in Hebrew, or god in Aramaic) of the skies

• Leningrad Codex: Yehvah elohei hashamayim (יְהוָה אֱלֹהֵי הַשָּׁמַיִם). Translation: Yehvah goddess (in Hebrew, or god in Aramaic) of the skies

Shamayim was a god worshiped by the Judahites until King Josiah banned his worship circa 625 BC. He appears to have been the primary god of the Samaritans until they were conquered by the Assyrians. Shamayim was the vaulted sky above the earth, where the sun, moon, and stars all moved around on tracks, according to the understanding of the world at the time.

King Cyrus II was a worshiper of Ahura Mazda, the Zoroastrian 'Lord of Wisdom.' Cyrus was accompanied into battle with an empty chariot in which Ahura Mazda was said to ride, which made the Persians victorious during campaigns. He would only have sent Nehemiah to Jerusalem to build a fire-temple if he believed that the Judahite Lord was Ahura Mazda. The Greek phrase appears to be a translation of the Zoroastrian title of Ahura Mazda: 'Lord-Master of the Universe.'

4 Codex Vaticanus: Nabouchodonosor (ΝΑΒΟΥΧΟΔΟΝΟϹΟΡ)

- Aleppo Codex: Nbwkdnṣr (נבוכדנצר)

- Leningrad Codex: Nevuchadnetzar (נְבוּכַדְנֶצַּר)

This is accepted as a reference to Nabû-kudurri-uṣur (𒀭𒀝𒋾𒂅𒊏𒉽𒋀), more commonly called Nebuchadnezzar II today, the king of the Neo-Babylonian Empire between 605 and 562 BC. Nebuchadnezzar II was the son of Nabû-apal-uṣur (𒀭𒀝𒌈𒇥𒋀), more commonly called Nabopolassar today, an Assyrian official who rebelled against Assyria in 626 BC. Nebuchadnezzar II was the chief architect of the Neo-Babylonian Empire, who in 605 BC, after taking the throne, launched an invasion of Assyria and Syria with his Median and Scythian allies, defeated the Assyrians and Egyptians, and incorporated Syria and Phoenicia into his Empire.

5 Codex Vaticanus: Mithridatou (ΜΙΘΡΑΔΑΤΟΥ)

- Aleppo Codex: Mtrdt (מתרדת)

- Leningrad Codex: Mitredat (מִתְרְדָת)

Mithradāta (𐎸𐎫𐎼𐎭𐎠𐎫) was a common name within the Persian and Median cultures, and several people with this name are recorded in close connection to Cyrus. The name means 'given by the deity Mithra,' which implies the families of these people were either Zoroastrians or Mithra worshipers, although the Persian royal family is always connected with Zoroastrianism. The name was later imported to Greek as Mithridatês (Μιθριδάτης), which was then adopted by the Romans as Mithridates, resulting in the English translation. The name used in the Septuagint's 2ⁿᵈ Ezra is not the Greek name, but a Greek transliteration of the Aramaic form of the name, supporting the Septuagint's book as being translated from an Aramaic text.

6 Codex Vaticanus: Sasabasar archonti tou Iouda (ϹΑϹΑΒΑϹΑΡ ΑΡΧΟΝΤΙ ΤΟΥ ΙΟΥΔΑ). Translation: Sasabasar ruler (or chief magistrate) of Judah

• Aleppo Codex: Ššbṣr hnšyå lYhwdh (שֵׁשְׁבַּצַּר הַנָּשִׂיא לִיהוּדה). Translation: Ššbṣr the prince (or president, chairman) of Judah

• Leningrad Codex: Sheshebatzar hannasi lYhudah (שֵׁשְׁבַּצַּר הַנָּשִׂיא לִיהוּדה). Translation: Sheshebatzar the prince (or president, chairman) of Judah

The name appears to be Babylonian šešab-sar (𒊩𒆷𒊬), meaning 'sea orchard,' suggesting that this was literal translation of the name of the Canaanite goddess Ôṯtrt-Ym (𒀀𒊏𒀜𒅀), meaning Asherah of the Sea. This goddess later called Astarte (Ἀστάρτη) by the Greeks, and had previously been banned by King Josiah, which would explain why the name was not translated by the Aramaic translators. It also indicates that this section of text originated in Neo-Babylonian cuneiform.

The person being mentioned in unclear, although he is the person that receives the treasures from the Temple of the Lord in both versions of Ezra. As Cyrus II released the Judahites, and did not attempt occupy Judah, it suggests that this was a Judahite prince that ruled between Cyrus' releasing the Judahites in 539 BC and Cambyses II's conquest of Southern Canaan in 526 BC. He disappeared from both Books of Ezra after receiving the treasures, which Zerubbabel later used to rebuild the temple. This has led some Christian groups to assume Sheshbazzar was another name for Zerubbabel, however, Zerubbabel was rebuilding the temple in 421 BC, during the reign of Darius II, more than a century after Sheshbazzar had been released by Cyrus II, making this explanation highly unlikely.

2nd Ezra: Chapter 2

These are the people of the land that went back from the number of prisoners who were taken captive, who King Nebuchadnezzar of Babylon took away to Babylon, and who returned to Judah and Jerusalem, each man to his city. Those who came with Zerubbabel: Jesus, Nehemiah, Seraiah, Reelaiah, Mordecai, Bilshan, Mizpar, Bigvai, Rehum, Baanah.

The number of the people of Israel:

The sons of Pharez: 2172.

The sons of Shephatiah: 372.

The sons of Arah: 775.

The sons of Phaathmoab, belonging to the sons of Jeshua Joab: 2812.

The sons of Elam: 1254.

The sons of Zattu: 945.

The sons of Zaccai: 760.

The sons of Bani: 642.

The sons of Bebai: 623.

The sons of Azgad: 1222.

The sons of Adonikam: 666.

The sons of Bigvai: 2056.

The sons of Adin: 454.

The sons of Ater of Hezekiah: 98.

The sons of Bezai: 323.

The sons of Jorah: 112.

The sons of Hashum: 223.

The sons of Gibbar: 95.

The sons of Bethlehem: 123.

The sons of Netophah: 56.

The sons of Anathoth: 128.

The sons of Azmaveth: 43.

The sons of Kirjath Arim, Chephirah, and Beeroth: 743.

The sons of Ramah and Geba: 621.

The men of Michmas: 122.

The men of Bethel and Ai: 423.

The sons of Nebo: 52.

The sons of Magbish, 156.

The sons of the other Elam:[1] 1254.

The sons of Elam: 320.

The sons of Lod, Aroth, and Ono: 725.

The sons of Jericho: 345.

The sons of Senaah: 3630.

The priests: the sons of Jedaiah, of the house of Jesus: 973.

The sons of Immer: 1052.

The sons of Pashhur: 1247.

The sons of Harim: 1007.

The Levites: the sons of Jesus and Kadmiel, belonging to the sons of Hodaviah: 74.

The sons of Asaph, the singers: 128.

The sons of the porters, the sons of Shallum, the sons of Ater, the sons of Talmon, the sons of Akkub, the sons of Hatita, and the sons of Shobai: in total 139.

The Nathins:[2] the sons of Ziha, the sons of Hasupha, the sons of Tabbaoth, the sons of Keros, the sons of Siaha, the sons of Padon, the sons of Lebanah, the sons of Hagabah, the sons of Akaboth, the sons of Hagab, the sons of Shalmai, the sons of Hanan, the sons of Giddel, the sons of Gahar, the sons of Reaiah, the sons of Rezin, the sons of Nekoda, the sons of Gazzam, the sons of Uzza, the sons of Paseah, the sons of Bezai, the sons of Asnah, the sons of Meunim, the sons of Nephusim, the sons of Bakbuk, the sons of Hakupha, the sons of Harhur, the sons of Bazluth, the sons of Mehida, the sons of Harsha, the sons of Barkos, the sons of Sisera, the sons of Tamah, the sons of Neziah, the sons of Hatipha.

The sons of the servants of Solomon: the sons of Sotai, the sons of Asepherath, the sons of Phadoura, the sons of Jaala, the sons of Darkon, the sons of Giddel, the sons of Shephatiah, the sons of Hattil, the sons of Pochereth - Aseboim, the sons of Ami. All the Nethins, and the sons of Abdeselma were 392.

These are those that traveled from Tel Melach,[3] Tel Charasha,[4] Cherub,[5] Edan,[6] and Immer.[7] They were not able to tell the house of their fathers, and their seed, whether they were of Israel: the sons of Delaiah, Boua, Tobiah,[8] and Nekoda: 652.

Of the sons of the priests: the sons of Habaiah, Koz, Barzillai who took a wife of the daughter of Barzillai the Gileadite, and was called by their name. Of these, their genealogy was not found although they had been searched for, and they were expelled from the priesthood. The military commander told them that they should not eat of the holiest things until the rising of a priest to shine a light on it and finalize it.[9]

All the congregation together were about 42,360, besides their slaves and woman-slaves, and these were 7337, and among these were 200 singing men and women. Their horses were 736, their mules were 245, their camels were 435, and their donkeys were 6720.

The chiefs of families, when they went into the Temple of the Lord that was in Jerusalem, offered willingly for the Temple of God, to establish it on its prepared place. According to their power, they gave into the treasury of the work, 61,000 pieces of pure gold, and 5000 pieces of silver, and one hundred priests' garments. So the priests, and the Levites, and some of the people, and the singers, and the porters, and the Nethins lived in their cities, and all Israel in their cities.

2ⁿᵈ Ezra: Chapter 2 Notes

1 Codex Vaticanus: Êlam - ar (ΗλΑΜ-ΑΡ)

- Aleppo Codex: Ôylm Åḥr (**עילם אחר**). Translation: Elam other

- Leningrad Codex: Eilam acher (**עֵילָם אַחֵר**). Translation: Elam other

As the Greeks transliterated 'Elam other' as a name, the original intent of the author is imported from the Masoretic text.

2 Codex Vaticanus: Nathinaeoe (ΝΑΘΙΝΑΙΟΙ)

- Aleppo Codex: Ntynym (**נתינים**)

- Leningrad Codex: Netinim (**נְּתִינִים**)

As the Greeks transliterated the Aramaic term, and therefore it is imported from the Masoretic Text. The Nathins were a group of temple slaves, believed to have not been of Israelite ancestry. It is believed that they dealt with the menial tasks at the temple for the priests. They were part of the temple retinue since Solomon built it.

3 Codex Vaticanus: Thelmeleth (ΘΕΛΜΕΛΕΘ)

- Aleppo Codex: Tl Mlh (**תל מלח**)

- Leningrad Codex: Tel Melach (**תֵּל מֶלַח**)

4 Codex Vaticanus: Thelarêsa (ⲐⲈⲖⲀⲢⲎⲤⲀ)

- Aleppo Codex: Tl Hršå (תל חרשא)

- Leningrad Codex: Tel Charsha (תֵּל חַרְשָׁא)

5 Codex Vaticanus: Charoub (ⲬⲀⲢⲞⲨⲂ)

- Aleppo Codex: krwb (כרוב). Translation: cherub (or griffin, sphinx)

- Leningrad Codex: keruv (כְּרוּב). Translation: cherub (or griffin, sphinx)

It should be noted that while Cherub, Addan, and Immer are treated as a series of names in this chapter of 2nd Ezra, and Masoretic Ezra-Nehemiah, this series of name has two other variants. In 1st Ezra, these are the names of three people, and Cherub is called Charaath (Χαρααθ). In the later Nehemiah sections of 2nd Ezra and the Masoretic Ezra-Nehemiah, the words read Cherub, ådwn (אדון) meaning 'lord,' and åmr (אמר) meaning 'said,' making the Nehemiah version 'Cherub lord said.'

If this was a geographic term, it could have been a reference to the Khabur River, or a settlement on it, where Ezekiel claimed to have seen Cherubs. This would explain why the Judahites in question could not trace their linage, as they would have been Samaritans that were relocated by the Assyrians. Cherubs were an iron age interpretation of the earlier bronze age Anatolian griffins, themselves based on Egyptian and Canaanite sphinxes.

6 Codex Vaticanus: Êdan (ⲎⲆⲀⲚ)

- Aleppo Codex: âdn (אדן). Translation: base

- Leningrad Codex: addan (אַדָּן). Translation: base

Later in the Nehemiah section of 2nd Ezra, the name is rendered as Êrôn (Ηρων), while in the Nehemiah section of Masoretic Ezra-Nehemiah, the word is âdwn (אדון), which translates as 'lord,' while the verse in 1st Ezra used Adan (Αδαν), which is the name of a person, not a location.

As there is no consensus, three different transliterations are used directly from the Greek, Adan in 1st Ezra, Edan in this verse, and Eron later in the Nehemiah version of this verse in chapter 17. Clearly, the confusion over what these three words mean long predates the Greek and Hebrew translations of Ezra-Nehemiah.

7 Codex Vaticanus: Emmêr (ⲈⲘⲘⲎⲢ)

- Aleppo Codex: âmr (אמר). Translation: said

- Leningrad Codex: Immer (אָמֵר)

The version of this name in 1st Ezra is Amar (Αμαρ), while the version in the Nehemiah section of 2nd Ezra is Iemêr (Ιεμηρ). The Masoretic words found in Ezra-Nehemiah are both âmr (אמר), and so Immer (אָמֵר) is used in this translation for both Emmêr (Εμμηρ) and Iemêr (Ιεμηρ) found in 2nd Ezra. Amar is used in 1st Ezra, as the three names are leaders, not places.

8 Codex Vaticanus: Tôbia (ⲦⲰⲂⲒⲀ)

- Aleppo Codex: Twbyh (טוביה)

- Leningrad Codex: Tovviyyah (טוֹבִיָּה)

In 1st Ezra, this man was called Touban (Τουβαν). 2nd Ezra is consistent in the spelling of the name in both the Ezra and Nehemiah sections. The Masoretic Ezra-Nehemiah spellings are likewise consistent with the spelling of the name. This appears to be a reference to Tobian Judahites (Τουβιανοὺς Ιουδαίους) mentioned in 2nd Maccabees, who were likely followers of the author of the book of Tobit, which was set in Assyria and Media.

9 Codex Vaticanus: eôs anastêi iereus toes phôtizousin cae toes telioes (ⲈⲰⲤ ⲀⲚⲀⲤⲦⲎⲒ ⲒⲈⲢⲈⲨⲤ ⲦⲞⲒⲤ ⲪⲰⲦⲒⲌⲞⲨⲤⲒⲚ ⲔⲀⲒ ⲦⲞⲒⲤ ⲦⲈⲀⲈⲒⲞⲒⲤ). Translation: until the rising of a priest to shine a light on it and finalize it.

- Aleppo Codex: ômd khn lÅwrym wlTmym (עמד כהן לאורים ולתמים). Translation: standing of the priest with the Urim and Thummim

- Leningrad Codex: amod kohen le'Urim uleTummim (עֲמֹד כֹּהֵן לְאוּרִים וּלְתֻמִּים). Translation: standing of the priest with the Urim and the Thummim

- 1st Ezra: anastêi archiereus endedymenos tên dêlôsin cae tên alêthian (ⲀⲚⲀⲤⲦⲎⲒ ⲀⲢⲬⲒⲈⲢⲈⲨⲤ ⲈⲚⲀⲈⲀⲨⲘⲈⲚⲞⲤ ⲦⲎⲚ

ⲆⲎⲀⲱⲤⲓⲚⲔⲀⲓⲦⲎⲚⲀⲁⲎⲑⲉⲓⲁⲛ). Translation: the rising of a high-priest dressed who could explain and not lie.

The Hebrew translations refer to the urim and thummim, artifacts that are believed to have been used for cleromancy in the Torah. They were used by the high priests in the books of the Kingdoms (Masoretic Samuel and Kings) and attached to the high-priest's breastplate. The term may translate as 'lights and perfections.'

2nd Ezra: Chapter 3

The seventh month began after the Israelites had returned to their cities, and the people assembled as one man in Jerusalem. Then Jesus ben Jehozadak, and his brothers the priests, and Zerubbabel ben Shealtiel, and his brothers, and they built the altar of the god of Israel, to offer on it whole burnt offerings, following that which was written in the law of Moses the prophet. They set up the altar on its place, and people of the lands were amazed, and the burnt offerings were offered to the Lord in the morning and in the evening. They kept the feast of tabernacles, following that which was written, and offered whole burnt offerings daily in number according to the ordinance, the exact daily rate. After this, burnt offerings continued for the new moon, and every sanctified feast, and every voluntary offering to the Lord.

On the first day of the seventh month, they began to offer burnt sacrifices to the Lord, before the foundation of the Temple of the Lord was laid. They gave money to the stone-masons and carpenters, and grains, drinks, and oil, to the Sidonians and Tyrians, to bring cedar trees from Lebanon to the sea by Jaffa, following the grant of King Cyrus of the Persians, which he granted them.

In the second year of their arrival at the Temple of God in Jerusalem, when the second month began, Zerubbabel ben Shealtiel, and Jesus ben Jehozadak, and the rest of their brothers the priests and the Levites, and all who came from the colony to Jerusalem appointed the Levites, from twenty years old and upward, over the craftsmen in the Temple of the Lord.

Jesus and his sons and his brothers stood, Kadmiel and his sons the Judahites, over those that worked the projets in the Temple of God, the sons of Henadad, their sons and their brothers the Levites. They laid a foundation for building the Temple of the Lord, and the priests carrying trumpets stood, and the Levites, the sons of Asaph with cymbals, to praise the Lord, following the order of King David of Israel. They sang with praise and thanksgiving to the Lord, "It's good! For centuries his mercy is on Israel!"

All the people declared with their voices great praise to the Lord at the foundation of the Temple of the Lord. Many of the priests and the Levites, and the archons, the tribal elders who had seen the first temple on its foundation, and who saw it no longer there, wept and cried loudly, but the crowd gleefully sang songs. The people did not distinguish the voice of the gleeful singing from the voice of the weeping of the people, for the people sang with a loud voice, and the voice was heard far away.

2nd Ezra: Chapter 4

Those who grieved Judah and Benjamin heard that the sons of the colony were building a temple for the Lord God of Israel. They approached Zerubbabel and the heads of families, and said to them, "We will build with you, as, like you do, we seek your god,[1] and we have sacrificed to him since the days that King Esarhaddon[2] of Assyria brought us here."

Then Zerubbabel and Jesus and the rest of the heads of the families of Israel said to them, "It is not for us to build a temple to our god with you. We will build together for the Lord God, as King Cyrus of the Persians commanded us."

The people of the land weakened the hands of the people of Judah, and hindered their building, hired people against them, and ploted to frustrate their counsel all the days of King Cyrus of the Persians, and during King Darius I[3] of the Persians.

In the reign of Xerxes I,[4] at the beginning of his reign, they wrote a letter against the inhabitants of Judah and Jerusalem.

In the days of Artaxerxes I, Tabeel wrote peaceably to Mithradates and the rest of his companions. The tribute-gatherer wrote to King Artaxerxes I[5] of the Persians in Aramaic[6] and interpreted it. Rehum the chancellor, and

Shimshai the scribe wrote a letter against Jerusalem to King Artaxerxes, saying:

"Rehum the chancellor has made a decision, and Shimshai the scribe, and the rest of our companions, the judges[7] and Persian supporters,[8] and the tax-collectors[9] of the Persians,[10] Urukians,[11] Babylonians, Susanians[12] (that is the Elamites),[13] and the rest of the nations who the great and noble Asennaphar[14] resettled in the cities of Samaria, and the rest of them beyond the river."

This is the letter which they sent to him:

"Your servants the men beyond the river to King Artaxerxes.

Let it be it known to the king, that the Judahites who traveled from you to us, have come to Jerusalem the rebellious and wicked city, which they are rebuilding, and its walls are being rebuilt, and they have established its foundations.

Now then, let it be known to the king, that if that city is rebuilt, and its walls completed, you will have no tribute, nor will they pay, and this hurts kings. It is not lawful for us to see the dishonor of the king, and therefore we have sent and made known the matter to the king, so examination may be made in your father's book of record. You will find, and you will know that the city is rebellious and does harm to kings and countries, and there are among it from ancient times refuges for runaway slaves, which is why this city has been made desolate.

We, therefore, declare to the king, that if that city is rebuilt and its walls are erected, you will not have peace."

Then the king replied to Rehum the chancellor, and Shimshai the scribe, and the rest of their companions who lived in Samaria, and the rest beyond the river, saying:

"Peace.

The tribute-gatherer who you sent to us, has been called before me. A decree has been made by me, and we have examined and found that that city in ancient times exalts itself against kings and that rebellions and desertions take place within it. There were powerful kings in Jerusalem, and they ruled over all the country beyond the river, and abundant revenues and tribute were given to them. Now, therefore, make a decree to stop the work of those men, and that city will no longer be built. See that you are careful in this decree, not to overlook this matter, or else at some time destruction could come and harm the kings."

Then the tribute-gatherer of King Artaxerxes read the letter before Rehum the chancellor, and Shimshai the scribe, and his companions, and they went quickly to Jerusalem and throughout Judah with horses and an armed force, and stopped them. At that time the work stopped on the Temple of God in Jerusalem, and it was paused until the second year of the reign of King Darius of the Persians.

2nd Ezra: Chapter 4 Notes

1 Codex Vaticanus: tô theô ymôn (ⲦⲰⲐⲈⲰ ⲨⲘⲰⲚ).
Translation: the god of yours

- Aleppo Codex: lålhykm (לאלהיכם). Translation: the god of yours

- Leningrad Codex: lEloheichem (לֵאלֹהֵיכֶם). Translation: the god of your

- Dead Sea Scroll 4QEzra: -ål- (-אל-). The word is very damaged, however, the surviving letters are in the correct position to have once been lålhykm (לאלהיכם).

2 Codex Vaticanus: Asaraddôn (ⲀⲤⲀⲢⲀⲆⲆⲰⲚ)

- Aleppo Codex: Åsr Hdn (אסר חדן)

- Leningrad Codex: Esar Chaddon (אֶסַר חַדֹּן)

Esarhaddon was the king of the Assyrian Empire between 681 and 668 BC. This reference to Esarhaddon settling people in the region, was likely after the rebellions of Sidon and Tyre in Lebanon. Judah was allied to Assyria at the time, and so the resettlement was not into the territory of Judah, however, but is possible that people were resettled in Samaria, which was part of the Assyrian Empire at the time, however, there are no other records of this.

3 Codex Vaticanus: Dariou (ⲆⲀⲢⲈⲒⲞⲨ)

- Aleppo Codex: Drywš (דריוש)

• Leningrad Codex: Dareyavesh (דָּרְיָוֶשׁ)

There were three Persian Kings named Darius: Darius I between 552 and 486 BC, Darius II between 423 and 404 BC, and Darius III between 336 and 330 BC. In this case, King Darius I (the Great) almost certainly is the king being referenced, as his reign was directly before Xerxes I, who is mentioned next.

4 Codex Vaticanus: Asouêrou (ΑϹΟΥΗΡΟΥ)

• Aleppo Codex: Åḥšwrwš (אחשורוש)

• Leningrad Codex: Achashverovosh (אֲחַשְׁוֵר֖וֹשׁ), generally anglicized as Ahasuerus.

Ahasuerus is the Hebrew name of Xšayārṣ̌ā (𐎧𐏁𐎹𐎠𐎼𐏁𐎠), today known as King Xerxes I, who ruled between 486 and 465 BC, and was the father of Artaxerxes I, who is mentioned in the next verse. Xerxes is Old Iranian for 'ruling over heroes,' which was translated into Babylonian as Aḫšiyaršu (𒄴𒅆𒅀𒅈𒋗), and then transliterated into Hebrew as Achashverovosh (אֲחַשְׁוֵר֖וֹשׁ). The English name Xerxes is derived from the Greek transliteration Xerxês (Ξέρξης), however, the translators working at the Library of Alexandria did not recognize the Aramaic name of Xerxes, and transliterated the name instead of translating it. The common English name Xerxes is used in this translation. There was also a Xerxes II, however, he only ruled for 45 days, and only established himself over the Persian heartland before being assassinated, and the people in Syria and Judea would have most likely not have heard of him. Ahasuerus was described favorably in later Judean writing, such as Esther, and according to this verse, did not do anything to stop Jerusalem from being rebuilt.

5 Codex Vaticanus: Arthasastha (ⲀⲣⲐⲀⳞⲀⳞⲐⲀ)

- Aleppo Codex: Ấrthŝŝtå (אַרְתְּחְשַׁשְׂתְּא)

- Leningrad Codex: Artachshasta K {artachshast Q}
(אַרְתַּחְשַׁשְׂתָּא כ {אַרְתַּחְשַׁסְתְּ ק})

This Artaxerxes could only have been Artaxerxes I, as he proceeded a Darius who allowed the work at the temple to continue. This Darius could not have been Darius I, Artaxerxes I's grandfather, and could not have been not Darius III, who was loosing his empire to the invading armies of Alexander the Great by year 2 of his reign. As the Darius has to have been Darius II, who ruled the empire between 423 to 404 BC, this Artaxerxes could only have been Artaxerxes I, who ruled the empire between, between 465 and 424 BC, a century after the text before it.

The stopping of the work on the walls of Jerusalem was likely tied to the rebellion in Egypt during Artaxerxes I's reign. Between 460 and 454 BC, a Libyan prince named Inaros II, who wanted to be the pharaoh of Egypt, led a revolt against Persian rule. In concert with Athenian allies, who invaded Anatolia at the time, he managed to capture all of Egypt south of Memphis (Cairo), before ultimately being defeated. This is a logical strategic reason for Artaxerxes I to rescind the orders of Cyrus II, which generally would not have been allowed under Persian law. This would date the events described to between 460 and 454 BC, years 5 through 11 of Artaxerxes I's rule.

6 Codex Vaticanus: Syristi (ⲥⲨⲣⲓⲥⲧⲓ). Translation: Syriac

• Aleppo Codex: Årmyt (ארמית). Translation: Aramaic

• Leningrad Codex: Aramit (אֲרָמִית). Translation: Aramaic

Syriac was the Greek name of the Aramaic language.

7 Codex Vaticanus: Dinaeoe (ⲇⲓⲛⲁⲓⲟⲓ)

• Aleppo Codex: dynyå (דינא)

• Leningrad Codex: dinaye (דִּינָיֵא)

This word is treated as a name in the Septuagint, however, is a transliteration of the Aramaic word dina (𐤃𐤉𐤍𐤀), meaning 'judge.'

8 Codex Vaticanus: apharsathachaeoe (ⲁⲫⲁⲣⲥⲁⲑⲁⲭⲁⲓⲟⲓ)

• Aleppo Codex: åprstkyå (אפרסתכיא)

• Leningrad Codex: afarsatchaye (אֲפַרְסַתְכָיֵא)

This term is debated, however, the traditional interpretation of the Hebrew texts is that it is a Persian title originally written in Aramaic. Paras (פָּרָס) is Hebrew and Aramaic for 'Persia,' while the second half of the word is the Persian word takja (تکیه) meaning 'support,' or 'supporter.' The generic term 'Persian supporters' is used in this translation, as that appears to have been the meaning of the original term.

9 Codex Vaticanus: tarphallaeoe (ΤΑΡΦΑΛΛΑΙΟΙ)

- Aleppo Codex: trplyå (טרפליא)

- Leningrad Codex: tarpelaye (טַרְפְּלָיֵא)

The term is generally debated and sometimes believed to be a title or a name of a place or people. The word appears to be a mistransliteration of tar-reôûm (𒋻𒉺𒇻), meaning 'divider of shepherds,' suggesting a tax-collector. The Babylonian word reôûm was spelled as sipa (𒉺𒇻) in cuneiform, itself composed of the glyphs PA (𒉺) and LU (𒇻), which the Aramaic translator appears to have transliterated directly. The letter was reported to have been written in Aramaic, and interpreted by the author Tabeel, suggesting it was a bilingual document.

The presence of mistransliterated Neo-Babylonian in the translation of the Aramaic, suggests that Tabeel was not fully fluent in Neo-Babylonian cuneiform. The older forms of cuneiform began to be marginalized outside of Mesopotamia from the era of Darius I (522 to 486 BC) onward, as he introduced a new form of cuneiform, today known as Old

Persian cuneiform. Based on the quadrilingual inscription of Artaxerxes I at the Reza Abbasi Museum in Teheran, it appears that the official languages and scripts of his empire were Old Persian cuneiform, Elamite cuneiform, Neo-Babylonian cuneiform, and Egyptian hieroglyphs, meaning that the Aramaic letter had to be 'interpreted' into one of these languages by Tabeel. Artaxerxes I faced numerous attempts at succession from the various regions of the empire, and his choice of Persian plus three regional languages was probably a compromise, however, it did not last, as the Aramaic script largely replaced cuneiform over the next century in Canaan and Mesopotamia.

10 Codex Vaticanus: apharsaeoe (ΑΦΑΡϹΑΙΟΙ)

• Aleppo Codex: åprsyå (אפרסיא)

• Leningrad Codex: afaresaye (אֲפָרְסָיֵא)

While this term is sometimes debated, it is generally accepted as the Greek and Hebrew transliterations of the Aramaic word for Prsy (ܦܪܣܝ), meaning 'Persians.' The Aramaic word also meant 'to divide,' as did it's cognate pršå (ܦܪܫܐ), which also meant 'cavalry' or 'horseman.' The more common translation of Persians is used as it fits the rest of the sentence.

11 Codex Vaticanus: Archyaeoe (ΑΡΧΥΑΙΟΙ)

* Aleppo Codex: Årkwy {Årkwyå} (אַרכוי {ארכויא})

* Leningrad Codex: Arkevai K {Arkevaye Q} (אָרְכְּוָי כ
{אָרְכְּוָיֵא ק})

This term is debated, however, is generally accepted as the Aramaic translations of Urukians, the people from the ancient city or Uruk (𒌷𒀕). The city of Uruk was a dominant city in southern Iraq in the Sumerian era, and continued to be a significant city until the Neo-Assyrian Empire annexed it circa 850 BC. Uruk was rebuilt and restored under the Neo-Babylonian Empire, and thrived under the Persian and Greek rules of the region, however, went into decline in the Parthian era, and never recovered.

12 Codex Vaticanus: Sousanachaeoe (ϹΟΥϹΑΝΑΧΑΙΟΙ)

* Aleppo Codex: Šwšnkyå (שׁוּשַׁנְכַיא)

* Leningrad Codex: Shushanchaye (שׁוּשַׁנְכָיֵא)

The Susanians were the people that had lived in Susa, the capital of Elam, before the Assyrians annihilated the country. The reference to them as separate from the Persians indicates that their culture had not been completely absorbed into the Persian culture when the letter was written, indicating it was early in the Persian era.

2ⁿᵈ Ezra: Chapter 4 Notes

13 Codex Vaticanus: dauaeoe Elamitae (ⲇⲁⲩⲁⲓⲟⲓ
ⲉⲗⲁⲙⲓⲧⲁⲓ)

* Aleppo Codex: dhwå {dhyå} Ôlmå (עלמיא **)דהיא{ דהוא**)

* Leningrad Codex: [dihu K] {dehaye Q} Elemaye ([כ **דהוא]**
(עֶלְמָיֵא {דְּהָיֵא} ק)

The Greeks seem to have mistranslated a scribal note as a reference to an otherwise unknown people. The Aramaic term dhyå (דְהָיְא) found in the Masorites Q source translates as 'who are.' The alternate reading of dhwå (דְהוא) in K source reads as 'who that' in Aramaic, however, may be the source of the Greek misreading, as while hwå (הוא) is the Hebrew term for 'is,' the d- (-ד) does not mean anything in Hebrew. This suggests the letter, or possibly the entire book of 2ⁿᵈ Ezra, had been translated into Judean-Aramaic, and the Greek translation was made from that translation. The scribal note indicates that the term ' Susanians' was not widely understood in Judea, and so the historic term was included.

14 Codex Vaticanus: Asennaphar (ⲁⲥⲉⲛⲛⲁⲫⲁⲣ)

* Aleppo Codex: Åsnpr (אסנפר)

* Leningrad Codex: Asenappar (אָסְנַפַּר)

This is sometimes theorized to be an ancient Aramaic reference to King Ashurbanipal, who ruled Assyria between 669 BC and 631 BC. Ashurbanipal spent the early years of his rule suppressing rebellions in Egypt, and later fought two campaigns against the Elamites, and devastated the country to

153

the point that the Persians were able to settle there and become the dominant culture within decades. He also fought a series of campaigns in the Arabian Peninsula and dominated most of northern Arabia. It is debated whether this is a reference to Ashurbanipal or one of his generals, and therefore the name Asennaphar is transliterated directly.

2nd Ezra: Chapter 5

Haggai the prophet with Zachariah ben Iddo, prophesied to the Judahites in Judah and Jerusalem in the name of the god in Israel. Then Zerubbabel ben Shealtiel rose up, and Jesus ben Jehozadak, and began to build the Temple of God that was in Jerusalem, and with them were the prophets of God assisting them.

In time Tattannu[1] the governor on this side of the river came to them, with Tishtrya-boznai,[2] and their companions, and asked them, "Who has ordained a decree for you to build this temple, and to provide for this work?"

They demanded, "What are the names of the men that build this city?"

But the eyes of God were on the colony of Judah, and they did not cause them to stop until the decree was taken to Darius, and then was sent by the tribute-gatherer concerning this.

The copy of the letter that Tattenai, the governor of this side of the river, and Tishtrya-boznai, and their companions the Persian supporters[3] who were on this side of the river, sent to King Darius II.[4] They sent the following:

"All peace to King Darius,

Let it be known to the king, that we went into the land

of Judea, to the temple of the great God,[5] and it is being built with choice stones, and they are laying timbers in the walls, and that work is progressing, and goes on well in their hands. We asked those elders, "Who gave you the order to build this temple, and to provide this preparation?" We asked them their names, in order to tell you, to write to you the names of their leading men.

They answered us, "We are the servants of the god of the sky and land, and we are rebuilding the temple which had been built many years before this. A great king of Israel built it and established it for them. But after that, our fathers provoked the god of the sky, he gave them into the hands of Nebuchadnezzar the Chaldean, king of Babylon, and he destroyed this temple and took the people as captives to Babylon. In the first year of King Cyrus, King Cyrus decreed that this Temple of God should be rebuilt. The gold and silver vessels of the Temple of God, which Nebuchadnezzar brought out from the temple that was in Jerusalem, and carried to the temple of the king, those King Cyrus brought out from the temple of the king, and gave them to Sheshbazzar the treasurer, who was in charge of the treasure, and said to him, "Take all the vessels, and go, and put them in the temple that is in Jerusalem in their place."

At that time, Sheshbazzar came and laid the foundations of the Temple of God in Jerusalem, and from that time until now, we have been building and has not been finished."

Now, if it seems good to the king, have a search made in the treasure-house of the king at Babylon, that you may know if it was a decree made by King Cyrus to rebuild the Temple of God that was in Jerusalem, and let the king reply to us when he has learned concerning this matter."

2ⁿᵈ Ezra: Chapter 5 Note

1 Codex Vaticanus: Thanthanai (ⲐⲀⲚⲐⲀⲚⲀⲒ)

- Aleppo Codex: Ttny (תתני)

- Leningrad Codex: Tattenai (תַּתְּנַי)

- 1ˢᵗ Ezra: Sisinnês (ⲤⲒⲤⲒⲚⲚⲎⲤ)

This is sometimes believed to be a reference to 'Tattenai, governor of Across-the-River,' the Satrap of Syria and Lebanon, who is recorded in cuneiform tablets dating to the year 502 BC, year 20 of Darius I's reign. Year 2 of Darius II was 421 BC, 81 years later, making this unlikely. Several cuneiform tablets bearing the name Tattenai have survived as part of what may have been a family archive, suggesting that the position of satrap in Syria and Lebanon may have been hereditary in the 5ᵗʰ century BC. The name used in this translation is normalized as Tattenai based on the name in 2ⁿᵈ Ezra, the Masoretic version of Ezra, and the cuneiform tablets.

2 Codex Vaticanus: Satharbouzana (ⲤⲀⲐⲀⲢⲂⲞⲨⲌⲀⲚⲀ)

- Aleppo Codex: Štr bwzny (שתר בוזני)

- Leningrad Codex: Shetar bozenai (שְׁתַר בּוֹזְנַי)

- 1ˢᵗ Ezra: Sathrabouzanês (ⲤⲀⲐⲢⲀⲂⲞⲨⲌⲀⲚⲎⲤ)

The meaning of the name is debated, however, it is accepted as being Old Persian. Phonetically, the name translates as 'Tishtrya delivers,' in Old Persian. Tishtrya was a rain and fertility deity/being in the Avesta, the Zoroastrian holy book, as a result, the name Tishtrya-boznai is used in this translation.

3 Codex Vaticanus: apharsachaeoe (ΑΦΑΡϹΑΧΑΙΟΙ)

This appears to be an alternate transliteration of the apharsathachaeoe (ΑΦΑΡϹΑΘΑΧΑΙΟΙ) in the previous chapter, which was the equivalent of the Hebrew term afarsatchaye (אֲפַרְסַתְכָיֵא), found in the Masoretic Text. This term is debated, however, the traditional interpretation of the Hebrew texts is that it is a Persian title originally written in Aramaic. Paras (פָּרַס) is Hebrew and Aramaic for 'Persia,' while the second half of the word is the Persian word takja (تکیه) meaning 'support,' or 'supporter.' The generic term 'Persian supporters' is used in this translation, as that appears to have been the meaning of the original term.

4 Codex Vaticanus: Dariô (ΔΑΡΕΙѠ)

* Aleppo Codex: Drywš (דריוש)

* Leningrad Codex: Dareyavesh (דָּרְיָוֶשׁ)

There were three Persian Kings named Darius: Darius I between 550 and 487 BC, Darius II between 423 and 404 BC, and Darius III between 380 and 330 BC. In this case, King Darius II is the only Darius that could be referenced, as he is the only Darius to reign after and Artaxerxes who could have authorized the continuation of the construction, as Darius III was loosing his empire to Alexander the Great's invading armies during his second year.

Additionally, this temple is later listed as being completed on the third day of the month of Adar in the sixth year of Darius, by which time Darius III was dead. The Passover Letter found within the Elephantine papyri confirms that Darius II was involved with the reconstruction of this temple, as it was sent in year 3 of Darius II, 418 BC.

5 Codex Vaticanus: theou tou megalou (ⲐⲈⲞⲨⲦⲞⲨ ⲘⲈⲄⲀⲖⲞⲨ). Translation: god that's great

• Aleppo Codex: ålhå rbå (אלהא רבא). Translation: goddess (in Hebrew, or god in Aramaic) great

• Leningrad Codex: Elaha rabba (אֱלָהָא רַבָּא). Translation: goddess (in Hebrew, or god in Aramaic) great

2nd Ezra: Chapter 6

After this, King Darius II decreed that a search should be made in the record-offices, where the treasure is stored in Babylon. There was found in the city, in the palace, a volume, and this is what was recorded in it. In the first year of King Cyrus, King Cyrus made a decree concerning the Temple of God that was in Jerusalem, saying,

> "Let the temple be built, and the place where they sacrifice the sacrifices. (Also he ordered its height at sixty cubits, and its width was at sixty cubits.) Let there be three strong layers of stone, and one layer of timber, and the expenses will be paid out of the house of the king. The silver and the gold vessels of the Temple of God, which Nebuchadnezzar carried off from the temple that was in Jerusalem, and carried to Babylon, let them even be given, and be carried to the temple that is in Jerusalem, and put in the place where they were set in the Temple of God.

Now, you rulers beyond the river, Tishtrya-boznai, and their companions the officers who are on the other side of the river, give these things, keeping far from that place. Leave alone the work of the Temple of God, and let the rulers of the Judahites and the elders of the Judahites build that Temple of God in its place. Also, I have made a decree, that you may help the elders of the Judahites in building that Temple of God, from out of the king's property, meaning the tributes beyond the river, let there be money to defray the expenses carefully granted to those men, so that they are not hindered.

Whatever needs there may be, you will give, both the young of bulls and rams and lambs for whole burnt offerings to the god of the sky, wheat, salt, wine, oil. Let it be given them according to the word of the priests that are in Jerusalem, day by day whatever they will ask, that they may offer sweet savors to the god of the sky and that they may pray for the life of the king and his sons.

A decree has been made by me, that every man who will alter this word, timber will be pulled down from his house, and let him be hung and killed on it, and his house will be confiscated. May the god whose name dwells there, overthrow every king and people who will stretch out his hand to alter or destroy the Temple of God which is in Jerusalem.

I, Darius have made a decree. Let it be diligently attended to."

Then Tattenai the governor on this side of the river, Tishtrya-boznai, and his companions, did diligently that which King Darius II sent. The elders of the Judahites and the Levites built, at the prophecy of Haggai the prophet, and Zachariah ben Iddo. They built up and finished it, by the decree of the God of Israel, and by the decrees of Cyrus, Darius, and Artaxerxes, kings of the Persians.

They finished this temple by the third day of Adar,[1] in the sixth year of the reign of King Darius II.[2] The

Israelites, the priests, and the Levites, and the rest of the sons of the colony kept the dedication of the Temple of God with joy. They offered for the dedication of the Temple of God a hundred calves, two hundred rams, four hundred lambs, and twelve goat kids for a sin-offering for all Israel, according to the number of the tribes of Israel. They set the priests in their divisions, and the Levites in their separate orders, for the services of the god in Jerusalem, according to the writing of the book of Moses.

The sons of the colony kept the Passover on the four-teenth day of the first month. For the priests and Levites were purified, all were clean to a man, and they killed the Passover sacrifice for all the sons of the colony, and for their brothers the priests, and for themselves. The Israelites ate the Passover, including those who were of the colony and everyone who separated himself to them from the uncleanness of the nations of the land, to serve the god the Lord of Israel. They kept the feast of unleav-ened bread seven days with gladness, because the Lord made them glad, and he turned the heart of the king of Assyria against them, to strengthen their hands in the works of the Temple of God in Israel.

2nd Ezra: Chapter 6 Notes

1 Codex Vaticanus: Adar (ᴧᴧᴧꝑ)

• Aleppo Codex: Ådr (אדר)

• Leningrad Codex: Adar (אֲדָר)

Adar is the twelfth month in the Hebrew Ecclesiastical calendar. The Hebrew Calendar is a lunisolar calendar, and so the months move somewhat in comparison to the Gregorian Calendar, and therefore the equivalent could be anywhere between February and April, depending on the year. However, Adar falls before the Northern Winter Equinox, and therefore March is the likely month being referenced.

2 As Darius I could not have restarted the work stopped by his grandson decades after his death, this must refer to Darius II, which would make the year 417 BC. The only other King Darius was Darius III, who died in his sixth year, and before the month of Adar. A letter from Zerubbabel's son Hananiah has survived from the year 418 BC, known as the Passover Letter, which states that Darius II had ordered the Judahites in Elephantine, Egypt, to observe the Passover, which confirms the interest in Zerubbabel's Temple.

2nd Ezra: Chapter 7

After this, during the reign of King Artaxerxes III[1] of the Persians, came Ezra ben Seraiah ben Azariah ben Hachaliah ben Shallum ben Zadok ben Ahitub ben Meraiah ben Azariah ben Meraioth ben Zerahiah ben Uzzi ben Bukki ben Abishua ben Phinehas ben Eleazar ben Aaron, the first priest.

Ezra left Babylon when he was already a scribe, quick with the Torah of Moses, which the Lord God of Israel gave, and the king gave him leave, for the hand of the Lord God was on him in all things which he did. Some of the Israelites traveled with him to Jerusalem in the seventh year of King Artaxerxes III, along with some of the priests, and Levites, and singers, and doorkeepers, and Nethins. They came to Jerusalem in the fifth month, in the seventh year of the king.

They left Babylon on the first day of the first month, and on the first day of the fifth month, they arrived in Jerusalem, as the good hand of his god was on him. Ezra had determined in his heart to seek the law and to do and teach the ordinances and judgments in Israel.

This is the copy of the order which Artaxerxes III gave to Ezra the priest, the scribe of the book of the words of the commandments of the Lord, and his ordinances to Israel:

"Artaxerxes, King of Kings, to Ezra, the scribe of the law

of the god of the sky,

Let the order and the answer be followed. A decree is made by me, that everyone in my kingdom from the people of Israel, and from the priests and Levites, who ar willing to go to Jerusalem, may go with you.

One has been sent from the king and the seven councilors, to visit Judea and Jerusalem, according to the law of their god that is in your hand. For the Temple of the Lord, there has been sent silver and gold, which the king and the councilors have freely given to the god of Israel, who resides in Jerusalem. All the silver and gold, whatever you will find in all the land of Babylon, with the donated offerings of the people, and the priests that offer freely for the Temple of God which is in Jerusalem. As for everyone that arrives there, speedily order him by this letter to bring calves, rams, lambs, and their meat-offerings, and their drink-offerings, and you will offer them on the altar of the temple of your god which is in Jerusalem.

Whatever seems good to you and to your brothers, do with the rest of the silver and the gold, do as it pleases your god. Deliver the vessels that are given you for the service of the Temple of God, before the god in Jerusalem. As to the rest of the needs of the temple of your god, you will give from the king's treasure-houses, and me, whatever seems good to you to give.

I, King Artaxerxes, have made a decree for all the treasuries that are in the land beyond the river, that whatever Ezra the priest and scribe of the god of the sky may ask you, it will be done quickly, to a limit of a hundred talents of silver, and a hundred measures of wheat, and a hundred vats of wine, and a hundred vats of oil, and salt without measure.

Let whatever is in the decree of the god of the sky, be done. Pay attention in case anyone attacks the temple of the god of the sky, or if there is anger against the realm of the king and his sons.

Also, this has been declared to you: Concerning all the priests, and Levites, the singers, porters, Nethins, and ministers of the Temple of God, let no tribute be paid to you, you will not have the power to oppress them.

You, Ezra, as the wisdom of God is in your hand, appoint scribes and judges, that they may judge for all the people beyond the river, all that know the law of your god, and you will make it known to him that doesn't know it. Whoever does not follow the law of God, and the law of the king readily, judgment will be taken against him, whether for death or chastisement, or a fine of his property, or thrown into prison."

Blessed is the Lord God of our fathers, who has put it this into the heart of the king, to glorify the Temple of the Lord which is in Jerusalem, and has given me favor in the eyes of the king, and of his councilors, and all the rulers of the king, the exalted ones. I was strengthened according to the good hand of God on me, and I gathered chief men of Israel to travel with me.

2nd Ezra: Chapter 7 Notes

1 Codex Vaticanus: Arthasastha (ΑΡΘΑϹΑϹΘΑ)

- Aleppo Codex: Årthšštå (אַרְתַּשַׁשְׂתְּא)

- Leningrad Codex: Artachshaste (אַרְתַּחְשַׁשְׂתְּא)

There were four kings named Artaxerxes that ruled the Persian Empire, however, this was almost certainly Artaxerxes III, and the year in question would have been 351 BC. The Artaxerxes in this verse could not have been Artaxerxes I, who stopped work on the Temple of God in chapter 4, as that the work at the temple did not continue until Darius II's reign. Artaxerxes IV only ruled for 2 years and the following verse refers to year 7 of Artaxerxes reign, so it could not have been him. The early years of Artaxerxes II's reign were spent in conflict with his cousin Cyrus the Younger over the throne, followed by a war against Sparta from 396 to 387 BC. Year seven of his reign would have been 397 BC, as the Spartan conflict was beginning to unfold, and it seems unlikely that he would have been focused on Jerusalem at the time. Later in his reign he lost a war to recapture the break-away state of Egypt, in 373 BC, and faced a revolt of the Satraps (governors) between 372 and 362.

Artaxerxes III inherited a diminished empire and spent the first few years of his reign fighting to restore order in Anatolia. In year 7 of his reign, 351 BC, he launched an invasion of Egypt, attempting to restore the land to the Persian Empire, however, after a year of fighting the Persians were defeated by the Egyptians and their Greek mercenaries. After the Persian defeat in Egypt, Anatolia, Cyprus, and Phoenicia quickly declared independence.

Notably, Jerusalem did not declare independence. The event described by Ezra, including the date and the xenophobia that Ezra enforced on the Judeans, fits well into this era, when the Persians were at war with the Egyptians, Greeks, and most of the peoples of Canaan, all of which Ezra had the Judeans evict from Judea. Artaxerxes spent the next few years brutally reoccupying the break-away regions, before launching another invasion of Egypt in 343 BC.

Judeans are reported to have been taken captive in Phoenicia, and relocated to Hyrcania, southeast of the Caspian Sea. Judeans were also relocated out of Egypt during the briefly restored Persian rule, and were resettled in Babylonia and Hyrcania, suggesting that Artaxerxes III considered the Judeans to be loyal to the empire.

2ⁿᵈ Ezra: Chapter 8

These are the heads of their families, the leaders that traveled with me in the reign of King Artaxerxes III of Babylon.

Of the sons of Phinehas: Gershom.

Of the sons of Ithamar: Daniel.

Of the sons of David: Hattush.

Of the sons of Shechaniah, and the sons of Parosh: Zachariah, and with him a brigade of 150.

Of the sons of Phaath-Moab: Elihoenai ben Zerahiah, and with him 200 men.

Of the sons of Zathoes: Shekaniah ben Jahaziel, and with him 300 men.

Of the sons of Adin: Ebed ben Jonathan, and with him 50 men.

Of the sons of Elam: Jeshaiah ben Athaliah, and with him 70 men.

Of the sons of Shephatiah: Zebadiah ben Michael, and with him 80 men.

Of the sons of Joab: Obadiah ben Jehiel, and with him 218 men.

Of the sons of Baani: Shelomith ben Josiphiah, and with him 160 men.

Of the sons of Bebai: Zachariah ben Bebai, and with him 28 men.

Of the sons of Azgad: Johanan ben Hakkatan, and with him 110 men.

Of the sons of Adonikam were the last, and these were their names: Eliphalat, Jeiel, and Shemaiah, and with them, 60 men.

Of the sons of Bigvai, Uthai, and Zabbud, and with him 70 men.

I gathered them to the river that was near Ahava, and we camped there three days while I reviewed the people and the priests, and found none of the Levites there. I sent men of understanding to Eleazar, Ariel, Shemaiah, Elnathan, Jarib, Elnatham, Nathan, Zachariah, Meshullam, Joiarib, and Elnathan. I forwarded them to the rulers with the money of the place, and I put words in their mouth to speak to their brothers, the Nethins, with the money of the place, that they should bring us singers for the temple of our god.

They came to us, as the good hand of our god was on us, even a man of understanding of the sons of Mahli, ben Levi, ben Israel, and at the commencement came to his sons and his brothers, numbering 18. Sherebiah, and Isaia of the sons of Merari, his brothers, and his sons, numbering 20. Of the Nethins, who David and the princes had appointed for the service of the Levites, there were 220 Nethins, all were gathered by their names.

I proclaimed there a fast, at the river Ahava, that we should humiliate ourselves before our god, to seek from him a straight path for us, and for our children, and for all our property. I was ashamed to ask from the king a guard and cavalry to save us from the enemy along the road, as we had spoken to the king, saying, "The hand of our god is on all that seek him for good, but his power and his anger are on all that abandon him."

So we fasted and asked of our god concerning this, and he listened to us. I gave orders to twelve of the chief priests to Zerahiah, Hashabiah, and ten of their brothers with them. I weighed for them the silver, and the gold, and the vessels of the first-fruits of the temple of our god, which the king, and his councilors, and his princes, and all Israel that were found, had dedicated. I even weighed in their hands 650 talents of silver, and 100 silver vessels, and 100 talents of gold, and 20 golden bowls, about 1000 darics,[1] and superior vessels of fine brass that shone like gold.

I said to them, "You saints of the lord, the vessels are sacred, and the silver and the gold are freely donated to the Lord God of our fathers. Be watchful and keep them until you weigh them before the chief priests, and the Levites, and the chiefs of families, in Jerusalem, at the chambers of the Temple of the Lord."

So the priests and the Levites took the weight of the silver, and the gold, and the vessels, to bring to Jerusalem to the Temple of God. We departed from the Ahava River on the twelfth day of the first month, to come to Jerusalem, and the hand of our god was on us and delivered us from the hand of enemies and adversaries along the road. We came to Jerusalem and stayed there for three days. On the fourth day that we weighed the silver, and the gold, and the vessels, in the Temple of God, by the hand of Meremoth ben Uriah the priest, and with him was Eleazar ben Phinehas, and with them Jehozabad ben Jesus, and Noadiah ben Bani, the Levites.

All things were calculated by number and weight, and the entire weight was written down. At that time the sons of the banishment that came from the colony offered whole burnt offerings to the God of Israel, 12 calves for all Israel, 96 rams, 77 lambs, 12 goats for a sin-offering, all whole burnt offerings to the Lord. They gave the king's mandate to the king's lieutenants, and the governors beyond the river, and they honored the people and the Temple of God.

2nd Ezra: Chapter 8 Notes

1 Codex Vaticanus: chilioe (ⲭⲓⲗⲓⲟⲓ). Translation: thousand

- Aleppo Codex: ǻdrknym ǻlp (אדרכנים אלף). Translation: darics thousand

- Leningrad Codex: adarchonim alef (אֲדַרְכֹנִים אֶלֶף). Translation: darics thousand

As the Greek text is not clear on the denomination, the term daric is imported from the Masoretic Text. The daric was the unit of currency in the Persian Empire.

2ⁿᵈ Ezra: Chapter 9

When these things were finished, the princes approached me, and said, "The people of Israel, and the priests, and the Levites, have not separated themselves from the people of the lands in their abominations, including the Canaanites, Greeks,[1] Perizzites, Jebusites, Ammonites, Moabites, Egyptians,[2] and Amorites. For they have taken of their daughters for themselves and their sons, and the holy seed has passed among the nations of the lands, and the hand of the rulers has been first in this transgression.

When I heard this, I tore my garments and trembled, and pulled on the hairs of my head and my beard, and sat down mourning. Then, there assembled around me all that followed the word of the God of Israel, on account of the transgression of the colony, and I remained mourning until the evening sacrifice.

At the evening sacrifice I rose up from my humiliation, when I had ripped my garments and I trembled, and I knelt on my knees, and spread out my hands to the Lord God, and said, "Lord, I am ashamed and confused, my God, to lift my face to you, for our transgressions have abounded over our head, and our trespasses have increased even to the sky. From the days of our fathers, we have been in a great trespass until today. Because of our iniquities, we, and our kings, and our children, have been delivered into the hands of the kings of the nations through the sword, and as captives, and as plunder, and with shame on our face, as like today.

Now our god has dealt mercifully with us, to leave us an escape, and to give us an establishment in the place of his sanctuary, to enlighten our eyes, and to give a little quickening in our servitude. For we are slaves, yet in our servitude, the Lord God has not deserted us, and he has extended favor to us in the sight of the kings of the Persians, to give us a quickening, that they should raise the Temple of God, and restore the desolate places of it, and to give us a fence in Judah and Jerusalem. What will we say, our god, after this?

We have forgotten your commandments, which you gave us through the hand of your servants the prophets, saying, 'The land, into which you go to inherit it, is a land subject to disturbance by the removal of the people of the nations for their abominations, where they have filled it from one end to the other by their uncleanness. Now, don't give your daughters to their sons, and don't take their daughters for your sons, neither will you seek their peace or their good, forever, that you may be strong, and eat the good of the land, and transmit it as an inheritance to your children, forever.'

After all that has come on us because of our evil deeds, and our great trespass, it is clear that there is none like our god, for you have visited our iniquities lightly, and given us deliverance, whereas we have repeatedly broken your commandments, and intermarried with the people of the lands. Do not be very angry with us to our complete destruction, so that there should be no remnant or one escaping. Lord God of Israel, you are righteous! We remain yet unpunished today! Look, we are before you in our trespasses! For we can't stand before you on this account!"

2nd Ezra: Chapter 9 Notes

1 Codex Vaticanus: Ethi (ϵΘι). Translation: tribes

- Aleppo Codex: Hty (חתי). Translation: Cypriots (or Greek)

- Leningrad Codex: Chitti (חִתִּי). Translation: Cypriots (or Greek)

The translators at the Library of Alexandria went to lengths to avoid translating the term 'Chitti,' as the 'Chitti' were generally the enemies in the ancient Israelite scriptures. In this case, the word was transliterated as Ethi (EΘι), in others it was Chettaion (Χετταίων). Kt (𐤊𐤕) and Kty (𐤊𐤕𐤉) were the Canaanite and Aramaic names of Cyprus during the Neo-Assyrian and Neo-Babylonian era, based on the name of the ancient Cypriot city-state, subsequently known as Cition (Κίτιον) in Greek. The name was recorded as Kåtjåy (𓈎𓏏𓇌𓈉) in Egyptian records from the New Kingdom Era in the late Bronze Age, and appears to have survived the Bronze Age Collapse better than most states. As the Aramaic term referred to the all Greek speaking lands by the Persian era, the translation of 'Greece' and 'Greeks' are used here.

2 Codex Vaticanus: Moseri (ΜΟϲϵρι)

- Aleppo Codex: Mṣry (מצרי). Translation: Egyptians

- Leningrad Codex: Mitzri (מִצְרִי). Translation: Egyptians

This transliteration of 'Egyptian' by the translators at the Library of Alexandria, is, like the previous transliteration of 'Greeks,' appears to be an attempt cover-up the fact that Ezra said the Greeks and Egyptians were unclean and should be rejected. It would not have gone over well at the Greco-Egyptian court of the Ptolemys, which controlled both Egypt and Cyprus at the time.

2nd Ezra: Chapter 10

After Ezra had prayed, and when he had confessed weeping and praying before the Temple of God, a great assembly of Israel came together to him, men and women and youths, for the people wept and wept aloud. Shekaniah ben Jeiel, of the sons of Elam, answered and said to Ezra, "We have broken the covenant with our god, and have taken foreign wives of the nations of the land, yet now there is patience and hope for Israel concerning this. Now then, let's make a covenant with our god, to divorce all the wives, and abandon their offspring, as you will advise. Rise, and alarm them with the commands of our god! Let it be done according to the law. Rise, for the matter, is on you, and we are with you. Be strong and do it!"

Then Ezra rose and ordered the rulers, priests, Levites, and all Israel, to swear that they would follow this word, and they swore. Ezra rose up from before the Temple of God, and went to the treasury of Johanan ben Eliashib. He went there, and he ate no bread and drank no water, for he mourned over the unfaithfulness of those of the colony. They made proclaimed throughout Judah and Jerusalem to all the sons of the colony, that they should assemble at Jerusalem, saying, "Everyone who will not arrive within three days, and take counsel with the rulers and the elders, all his property will be forfeited, and he will be separated from the congregation of the colony."

So all the men of Judah and Benjamin assembled at Jerusalem within the three days. This was the ninth month. On the twentieth day of the month, all the people sat down in the street by the Temple of the Lord, because of their alarm concerning the word, and because of the storm. Ezra the priest arose, and said to them, "You have broken the covenant, and have taken foreign wives, to add to the trespass of Israel. Now, therefore, praise to the Lord God of our fathers, and do that which is pleasing in his sight, and separate yourselves from the peoples of the land, and from the foreign wives."

Then all the congregation answered and said, "This, your word is powerful on us to do it. But the people are many, and the season is stormy, and there is no strength to stand outside, and the work is more than one or two days, as we have greatly sinned in this matter. Let our rulers stand for now, and for all those in our cities who have taken foreign wives, let them come at appointed times, and with them, elders from every city, and judges, to turn away the fierce anger of our god from us concerning this matter."

Only Jonathan ben Asahel, and Jahaziah ben Tekoah were with me regarding this, and Meshullam, and Sabbathai the Levite helped them.

The sons of the colony did this, and Ezra the priest, and heads of families according to their house were separated, and all by their names, for they returned on the first day of the tenth month to search out the matter. They made an end to all the men who had taken foreign wives by the first day of the first month, and there were found some of the sons of the priests who had taken foreign wives.

Of the sons of Jesus ben Jehozadak, and his brothers: Maaseiah, Eliezer, Jarib, and Gedaliah. They pledged themselves to divorce their wives and offered a ram of the flock for a trespass-offering because of their trespass.

Of the sons of Immer: Hananiah, and Zebadiah.

Of the sons of Harim: Maaseiah, Elijah, Shemaiah, Jeiel, and Uzziah.

Of the sons of Phasur: Elioenai, Maaseiah, Ishmael, Nethaneel, Jehozabad, and Elasah.

Of the Levites: Jehozabad, Shemaiah, Kelaiah (he is Kelita,) Pethahiah, Judah, and Eliezer.

Of the singers: Eliashib: and of the porters; Shallum, Telem, and Oduth.

Also of Israel: of the sons of Parosh: Ramiah, Uzziah, Malchiah, Miniamin, Eleazar, Hashabiah, and Bani.

Of the sons of Elam: Mattaniah, Zechariah, Jehiel, Obadiah, Jeremoth, and Elijah.

Of the sons of Zattu: Elioenai, Eliashib, Mattaniah, Jeremoth, Zabad, and Aziza.

Of the sons of Babei: Johanan, Hananiah, Zabbai, and Athlai.

Of the sons of Bani: Meshullam, Malluch, Adaiah, Jashub, and Sheal, and Meremoth.

Of the sons of Pahathmoab: Adna, and Chelal, and Bani, Maaseiah, Mattaniah, Bezaleel, and Bani, and Manasseh.

Of the sons of Harim: Eliezer, Jesaiah, Malchiah, Shemaiah, Shimeon, Benjamin, Baluch, Samaria.

Of the sons of Hashum: Mattaniah, Mattathah, Zabad, Eliphelet, Jeremai, Manasseh, Shemaiah.

Of the sons of Bani: Moadiah, Amram, Uel, Bani, Bedeiah, Chelluh, Vaniah, Meremoth, Eliashib, Mattaniah, and Mattaniah, and from the sons of Bani, and the sons of Shemaiah: Shelemiah, Nathan, Adaiah, Machnadebai, Shashai, Sharai, Azareel, and Shelemiah, and Samaria, and Shallum, Meraiah, and Joseph.

Of the sons of Nebo: Jeiel, Mattaniah, Zabad, Zebina, Jadau, and Joel, and Bani.

All these had taken foreign wives and had fathered sons with them.

2nd Ezra: Chapter 11

The words of Nehemiah ben Hachaliah.

It happened in the month of Kislev,[1] in the twentieth year,[2] that I was in Susa[3] at the palace. Hananiah, one of my brothers, came, with some men from Judah, and I asked them regarding those that had escaped, who had been left of the colony, and concerning Jerusalem. They answered me, "The remnant, including those that are left of the colony, are there in the land, in great distress and reproach, and the walls of Jerusalem are pulled down, and its gates are burnt with fire."

When I heard these words I sat down and wept, and mourned for several days, and continued fasting and praying before the god of the sky. I said, "No, I beg you, Lord God of the sky, the mighty, the great and terrible, keep your covenant and have mercy on those that have affection for you, and to those that keep your commandments, let your ear listen, and your eyes open, that you may hear the prayer of your servant, which I pray before you at this time, this day both day and night, for the Israelites your servants, and make confession for the sins of the Israelites, which we have sinned against you, both I and the house of my father have sinned. We have altogether broken the covenant with you, and we have not kept the commandments, and the ordinances, and the judgments, which you did command your servant Moses."

"Remember, I beg you, the word where you ordered your servant, Moses, 'If you break the covenant with me, I will disperse you among the nations. But if you return again to me, and keep my commandments, and do them, even if you should be scattered under the distant edges of the sky, there will I gather them, and I will bring them into the place which I have chosen to cause my name to live there.' Now they are your servants and your people, whom you have redeemed with your great power, and with your strong hand. Don't turn away, I beg you, Lord, but let your ear listen to the prayer of your servant, and to the prayer of your servants, who desire to fear your name, and prosper, I beg you, your servant this day, and cause him to find mercy in the sight of this man."

At the time, I was the king's cupbearer.

2nd Ezra: Chapter 11 Notes

1 Codex Vaticanus: Chaseêlou (ⲬⲀⲤⲈⲎⲀⲞⲨ)

* Aleppo Codex: Kslw (כסלו)

* Leningrad Codex: Kislev K {Kisleiv Q} (כִּסְלֵו כ {בִּכְסְלֵיו ק})

Kislev is the ninth month of the Hebrew Ecclesiastical calendar. The Hebrew Calendar is a lunisolar calendar, and so the months move somewhat in comparison to the Gregorian Calendar, and therefore the equivalent could be anywhere between November and December.

2 This is identified later as the 20th year of Artaxerxes, which can only be Artaxerxes II, making the year 384 BC. Artaxerxes I did reign more than 20 years, however, he is reported in chapter 4 as having stopped the work at the temple in Jerusalem, likely during the Egyptian rebellion of his 5th through 11th years (460-454 BC). It is later reported that work did not resume at the temple until the reign of Darius, so it could not have been him. Artaxerxes III died in his twentieth year, but before the month of Kislev, and Artaxerxes IV only ruled for 3 years, so it could not have been either of them.

The twentieth year of Artaxerxes II's reign, was three years after the end of the very expensive Corinthian War against Sparta, in which the Persians spent massive amounts of money subsidizing the Greek states that were part of the anti-Spartan league, including the Athenians, Thebans, and Corinthians. The peace treaty was concluded in his 18th year (386 BC), and stabilized Anatolia for a couple of decades. In year 19, he fought the Cadusian campaign in modern northwest Iran, which suppressed an attempted rebellion. In the 20th year of Artaxerxes rule, he was between conflicts, after having stabilized most of the empire. The only major issue he had not resolved was Egypt, which had successfully broken away from Persian control in 404 BC when he had assumed the throne. By his 27th year (377 BC), he began preparing for the invasion of Egypt, which resulted in the massive invasion in his 31st year (373 BC), involving more than 200,000 Persian soldiers, and was a complete failure. This weakened the empire and led to the Satraps (governors) rebelling the following year (372 BC), which took a decade to suppress. During the Satrap rebellion, Egypt and Sparta jointly invaded Phoenicia in an attempt to liberate the land. It is unclear if they approached Jerusalem, however, the Persians did ultimately defeat the Spartans and Egyptians.

Artaxerxes II's investment in Jerusalem in 384 BC, and specifically, the rebuilding of the walls, appears to be part of his larger plans to reconquer Egypt, or at least to defend Judea against an Egyptian invasion.

3 Codex Vaticanus: Sousan (ⲥⲟⲩⲥⲁⲛ)

- Aleppo Codex: Šwšn (שׁוּשַׁן). Translation: Susa

- Leningrad Codex: Šûšan (שׁוּשַׁן). Translation: Susa

The city of Susa, in southern modern Iran, was the winter capital of the Persian Empire from the era of Darius I onward.

It had been the capital of the Elamite kingdom before Cyrus II conquered them.

2nd Ezra: Chapter 12

It happened in the month of Nisan, in the twentieth year of King Artaxerxes II, that the wine was before me, and I took the wine and gave it to the king, and there was not another before him. The king asked me, "Why are you so sad? Can you not control yourself? Now, this is nothing but sorrow of heart."

Then I was extremely alarmed, and replied to the king, "Let the king live forever! Why should I not be sad, when the city and the home of the sepulchers of my fore-fathers, has been laid waste, and her gates have been burnt with fire?"

The king asked me, "For what do you ask?"

So I prayed to the god of the sky, and I said to the king, "If it seems good to the king, and if your servant will have found favor in your sight, I ask that you would send him to Judah, to the city of the sepulchers of my fore-fathers, so I will rebuild it."

The king and his concubine that sat next to him asked me, "How long will your journey be, and when will you return?"

The proposal was pleasing to the king, and he sent me away, and I appointed him a time. I said to the king, "If it seems good to the king, let him give me letters to the governors beyond the river, to forward me until I come to Judah, and a letter to Asaph the keeper of the forest which belongs to the king, that he may give me timber to cover the gates, and for the wall of the city, and for the house into which I will enter."

The king gave to me accordingly, as the good hand of God was on me. I came to the governors beyond the river, and I gave them the king's letters. (Now the king had sent with me captains of the army and cavalry.) Sanballat the Aaronite[1] heard it, and the slave[2] Tobiah the Ammonite, and it was terrible to them that a man had come seeking good for the Israelites.

I arrived in Jerusalem and was there for three days. I rose up at night, I and a few men with me, and I told no man what God put into my heart to do with Israel. There were no animals with me, except the animal I rode on. I went out by the gate of the valley at night, and to the mouth of the well of fig trees, and the dung-gate, and I mourned over the wall of Jerusalem which they had destroyed, and her gates that were burnt with fire. I traveled on to the fountain gate, and the king's pool, and there was no room for the animal to pass under me. I went up along the wall of the brook at night, and mourned over the wall, and passed through the gate of the valley, and returned.

The sentinels did not know why I went, or what I was doing, and until that time I did not tell the Judahites, or the priests, nobles, captains, or to the rest of the men who worked the works. Then I said to them, "You see this evil, in which we are, how Jerusalem is desolate, and her gates have been burnt by fire. Come, and let's rebuild the wall of Jerusalem, and we will be no longer an insult. I told them of the hand of God which was good on me, also about the words of the king which he spoke to me, and I said, "Let's rise and build," and their hands were strengthened for the good work.

Sanballat the Aaronite, and the slave Tobiah the Ammonite, and Geshem the Arabian heard it and they laughed insulting us, and came to us, asking, "What is this thing that you are doing? Are you revolting against the king?"

I answered them, "The god of the sky will help us, and we, his servants, are pure and we will build. But you have no part, or right, or memory in Jerusalem."

2ⁿᵈ Ezra: Chapter 12 Notes

1 Codex Vaticanus: Arôni (ικωρΑ)

- Aleppo Codex: ḥrny (חרני)

- Leningrad Codex: Choroni (חֹרֹנִי)

This term is debated, however, the Hebrew version is likely a transliterated Aramaic term for someone from Harran, the ancient Assyrian city, where Samaritans had been relocated to during the Neo-Assyrian era. The city had been named Harran since the Sumerian era, called Ḥarraan (𒄷𒊏) in Sumerian, and Harrânu (𒈗) in Akkadian, Assyrian, and Babylonian. In Hebrew, the name of the city was Haran (הָרָן), and Armenian it was Haran (Խառան), however, the term in the Masoretic text is not the proper Hebrew term for someone from Harran, and the Greeks could not have recognized the term they translated as referring to someone from Harran, as the Greek translation of Harran was Carrhae (Κάρραι).

The Greek term appears to be a transliteration of the Aramaic spelling of Aharoni (אַהֲרוֹנִי), meaning 'descendant of Aaron,' which would mean that it was an alternate term to 'Levite.' As Sanballat the Arôni / Ḥōrōnî is a leader of the Samaritans, it could also be an intentional corruption of the two terms by the Hebrew translator, to indicate that Sanballat was not a real Aḥărônî, but a Harranian. At the end of 2ⁿᵈ Ezra, the author claims that the Arôni/Ḥōrōnî broke the covenant of the Levites, which supports this reading. As the Greek transliteration appears to be closer to Aaron than Carrhae, the translation of Aaronite it used.

2 Codex Vaticanus: doulos (ⲇⲟⲩⲗⲟⲥ). Translation: slave (or subservient)

- Aleppo Codex: ôbd (עבד). Translation: servant (or slave)

- Leningrad Codex: ebed (עֶבֶד). Translation: servant (or slave)

This Tobiah was represented in some lines as being an influential person, and so the term 'slave' is likely being used as an insult, as it was at the time.

2nd Ezra: Chapter 13

Then Eliashib the high priest, and his brothers the priests rose up, and rebuilt the sheep-gate. They sanctified it and set up the doors of it, and also the tower of the hundred, and they sanctified the tower of Hananeel. They rebuilt by the side of the men of Jericho, and by the side of the sons of Zaccur, ben Imri. The sons of Senuah built the fish-gate, they roofed it and covered over its doors, and bolts, and bars.

Next to them the order reached to Meremoth ben Uriah, ben Koz, and next to them Meshullam son of Berechiah ben Meshezabeel took his place, and next to them Zadok ben Baanah took his place. Next to them, the Tekoites took their place, but the Adorim did not apply their necks to their service. Jedaiah ben Paseah, and Meshullam son of Besodeiah repaired the old gate. They covered it in and set up its doors, and its bolts, and its bars.

Next to them worked Melatiah the Gibeonite, and Evaron the Meronothite, the men of Gibeon and Mizpeh, to the throne of the governor on this side the river. Next to him Azarael ben Harhaiah of the smiths, carried on the repairs, and next to them Hananiah ben one of the apothecaries repaired, and they finished Jerusalem to the broad wall. Next to them worked Rephaiah ben Hur, the ruler of half the district around Jerusalem.

Next to them worked Jedaiah ben Harumaph, and in front of his house and next to him worked Hattush son of Hashabniah. Next to him worked Malchiah ben Harim, and Hashub ben Pahathmoab, all the way to the tower of the furnaces. Next to him worked Shallum ben Halohesh, the ruler of half the district around Jerusalem, along with his daughters. Hanun and the inhabitants of Zanoah repaired the gate of the valley. They built it and set up its doors, and its bolts, and its bars, and a thousand cubits of the wall as far as the dung-gate.

Malchiah ben Rechab, the ruler of the district around Beth Haccerem, repaired the dung-gate, he and his sons. They covered it, and set up its doors, and its bolts, and its bars. But Solomon ben Colhozeh repaired the gate of the fountain, the ruler of part of Mizpeh. He built it, and covered it, and set up its doors and its bars, and the wall of the pool of the skins by the meadow of the king, and as far as the steps that lead down from the City of David.

Beyond him, Nehemiah son of Azbuk, ruler of half the district around Beth Zur, repaired as far as the garden of David's sepulcher, and as far as the artificial pool, and as far as the house of the mighty men. Beyond him, the Levites worked, including Rehum ben Bani. Next to him worked Hashabiah, ruler of half the district around Keilah, in his district. Beyond him, his brothers, Bavai son of Henadad, ruler of half the district around

Keilah worked. Next to him worked Azzur ben Joshua, ruler of Mizpah, another portion of the tower of ascent, where it meets the corner.

Beyond him, worked Baruch ben Zabbai, a second portion, from the corner as far as the door of the house of Eliashib the high priest. Beyond him, Meremoth ben Uriah ben Koz, a second part from the door of the house of Eliashib, to the end of the house of Eliashib repaired. Beyond him, the priests worked, the men of Ecchechar. Beyond him, worked Benjamin and Hashub near their house, and beyond him worked Azariah son of Maaseiah ben Hananiah on the parts near to his house.

Beyond him, worked Bani ben Hadad, another portion from the house of Azariah as far as the corner and to the turning, of Palal ben Uzai, opposite the corner, and where is also the tower that projects from the king's house, even the upper one of the prison-house, and beyond him worked Pedaiah ben Parosh.

The Nethins lived in Ophel, as far as the garden of the water-gate eastward, and there is the projecting tower. Beyond them, the Tekoites repaired another portion opposite the great projecting tower, even as far as the wall of Ophla. The priests repaired above the horse-gate, every man near his own house. Beyond him, Zadok ben Immer repaired opposite his own house, and beyond him repaired Shemaiah son of Shechaniah, guard of the east-gate.

Beyond him, Hananiah son of Shelemiah worked, and Hanun, the sixth son of Zalaph, on another portion beyond him, and Meshullam ben Berechiah worked over near his treasury. Beyond him, Malchiah ben Sarephi worked as far as the house of the Nethins, and the merchants over near the gate of Miphkad, and as far as the steps of the corner. Between that and the sheep-gate, the smiths and merchants worked.

2ⁿᵈ Ezra: Chapter 14

When Sanballat heard that we were building the wall, it sounded terrible to him, and he was very angry and lobbied against the Judahites. He said before his brothers (that is the army of the Samaritans), "Is it true that these Judahites are rebuilding their city? Do they again offer sacrifices? Will they succeed? Will they today restore the stones, after they have been burnt and made a heap of rubbish?"

Tobiah the Ammonite approached him, and said to them, "Do they sacrifice or eat in their place? Won't a fox go up and pull down their wall of stones? Listen, our god, for we have become an insult! Return their reproach on their head, and make them an insult in a land of their captivity, and do not cover their iniquity."

But it happened that when Sanballat and Tobiah, and the Arabians, and the Ammonites, heard that the building of the walls of Jerusalem was proceeding and that the holes began to be repaired, it seemed very terrible to them. All of them assembled to come to fight against Jerusalem, and to destroy it completely. So we prayed to our god and set watchmen against them day and night, because of them.

Judah said, "The strength of the enemies is broken, yet there is much rubbish, and we will not be able to rebuild the wall."

Those who afflicted us said, "They will not know, and they will not see, until we advance into the middle of them, and kill them, and cause the work to stop."

The Judahites who lived near them came and told us, "They are coming up against us from every quarter."

So I set men in the lowest part of the place behind the wall in the lurking-places, I even set the people according to their families, with their swords, their spears, and their bows. I looked, and arose, and said to the nobles, and to the captains, and to the rest of the people, "Do not be afraid of them! Remember our great and terrible god, and fight for your brothers, your sons, your daughters, your wives, and your houses."

When our enemies heard that it was made known to us, and God had frustrated their plans, we all returned to the wall, every man to his work. From that day half of them that had been driven out, worked the work, and half kept guard, and there were spears, and shields, and bows, and breastplates, and rulers behind the whole house of Judah, even those who were building the wall. Those who carried the burdens were under arms, each with one hand worked his work, and with the other on his lance.

The builders worked each man having his sword strapped to his waist, and so they built, and the trumpeter with his trumpet next to him. I said to the nobles, and to the rulers, and to the rest of the people, "The work is great and abundant, and we are spreading out along the wall, each at a great distance from his brother. In whatever place you will hear the sound of the cornet, there gather yourselves together to us, and our god will fight for us."

So we continued laboring at the work, and half of them held the spears from the rising of the morning until the stars appeared. At that time I said to the people, "Every man among you should lodge in Jerusalem with his servants, and let the night be a watch-time for you, and the day a work-time."

I was there, and the watchmen behind me, and there was not a man of us that took off his clothes.

2nd Ezra: Chapter 15

The cry of the people and their wives was great against their brothers the Judahites. Some said, "We are numerous with our sons and our daughters, so we will take grain, and eat and live."

Some said, "Let us pledge our fields and vineyards and houses, and we will take grain and eat."

Some said, "We have borrowed money for the king's tributes, and our fields, and our vineyards, and houses are already pledged. Now our flesh is as the flesh of our brothers, our children are like their children, yet, look, we are reducing our sons and our daughters to slavery, and some of our daughters are enslaved, and there is no power left in our hands, as our fields and our vineyards belong to the nobles."

I was greatly saddened when I heard their cry and these words. My heart took counsel within me, and I contended against the nobles and the princes, and I said to them, "Should every man demand of his brother what you demand?"

I appointed against them a great assembly, and I said to them, "We the free, have redeemed our brothers the Judahites that were sold to the nations, yet you sell your brothers? Will they be returned to us?"

They were silent and found no answer. I continued, "The thing that you do is not good. You do not walk in the fear of our god, because of the reproach of the nations our enemies. Both my brothers, and my acquaintances, and I have lent them money and grain. Let's now abandon this debt. Restore to them, I beg, today, their fields, and their vineyards, and their olive yards, and their houses, and give them grain and wine and oil, from the money."

They answered, "We will restore, and we will not demand payment from them. We will do this as you say."

Then I called the priests and bound them by oath to do according to this word. I shook out my garment, and said, "May God shake out every man who will not keep to this word, from his house, and from his labors, he will be shaken out like this as an outcast and abandoned."

All the congregation replied, "Amen," and they praised the Lord, and the people did this thing.

From the day that he ordered me to be their ruler in the land of Judah, from the twentieth year even to the thirty-second year of Artaxerxes II,[1] twelve years, I and my brothers did not eat provisions extorted from them. But as for the former acts of extortion in which those who were before me oppressed them, they even took from them their last money, forty shekels[2] for bread and wine, and the very outcasts of them exercised authority over the people. I did not do so, because of the fear of God. Also, in the work on the wall, I didn't treat them strictly, I bought no land, and all that were gathered together came there to the work.

The Judahites, up to 150 men, besides those coming to us from the nations, were at my table. There came to me each day one calf, and I had six choice sheep and a goat, and every ten days wine in abundance of all sorts. Yet, I did not acquire the food through extortion because slavery was heavy on these people. Remember me, God, as good, in all that I have done to these people.

2nd Ezra: Chapter 15 Notes

1 Only two Persian kings named Artaxerxes ruled for more than 32 years: Artaxerxes I, who ruled for 41 years, and Artaxerxes II, who ruled for 46 years, and as Artaxerxes I had stopped the work on the temple, which was not continued until the time of Darius II, and it could not have been continued during the reign of Darius III, this confirms the king was Artaxerxes II. Year 32 of Artaxerxes II's reign was 372 BC, the year the Revolt of the Satraps began, after the failed invasion of Egypt. Nehemiah's returning to the king, suggests he helped to suppress the revolting satraps, and that the king had temporarily halted his plans to reoccupy Egypt.

2 Codex Vaticanus: didrachma (ΔΙΔΡΑΧΜΑ). Translation: two-drachma

- Aleppo Codex: šqlym (שְׁקְלִים). Translation: shekels

- Leningrad Codex: shekalim (שְׁקָלִים). Translation: shekels

The shekel was a unit of weight used throughout the Middle East for thousands of years, believed to originate during the Akkadian era as the šiqlum (𒅆). It weighed approximately 8.6 grams of silver. The Greek drachma was a coin weighing approximately half a shekel, and therefore under Greek rule of the Middle East, a two-drachma coin was used. As the Greeks clearly translated shekel into didrachma, the term shekel is restored in this translation.

2nd Ezra: Chapter 16

When Sanballat, Tobiah, and Geshem the Arabian, and the rest of our enemies, heard that I had built the wall, and that there was no opening left in it, (but until now I had not set up the doors on the gates,) then Sanballat and Geshem sent a message to me, saying, "Come and let's meet together in the villages in the plain of Ono,"[1] but they were plotting to attack me.

I sent messengers to them, saying, "I am doing great work, and I will not be able to come, or else the work could stop. As soon as I have finished it, I will come to you."

They sent to me again asking the same thing, and I sent them the same reply. Then Sanballat sent his servant to me with an open letter in his hand. In it was written:

> "It has been reported among the nations that you and the Judahites are planning to revolt, therefore you are building the wall, and you will be a king over them. Moreover, you have appointed prophets for yourself, that you might live in Jerusalem like a king over Judah, and now these words will be reported to the king. Now then, come, let's discuss things."

I sent a messenger to him, saying:

> "It has not happened according to these words that you say, and you frame them falsely out of your heart."

All were trying to alarm us, saying, "Their hands will be weakened from this work, and it will not be done."

Then, therefore, I strengthened my hands. I went into the house of Shemaiah ben Delaiah ben Mehetabel, and he was locked in. He said, "Let us assemble together in the Temple of God, in the middle of it, and let's shut its doors, as they are coming at night to kill you."

I said, "Who is the man that will enter into the temple, and may live?"

I watched and found God had not sent him, for the prophecy was a lie devised against me, and Tobiah and Sanballat had hired many against me, that I might be frightened, and do this, and sin and become to them an ill name, that they might insult me. Remember, God, Tobiah and Sanballat, according to these their deeds, and the prophetess Noadiah, and the rest of the prophets who tried to scare me.

The wall was finished on the twenty-fifth day of Elul,[2] in fifty-two days. It happened, when all our enemies heard of it, that all the nations around us were afraid, and great alarm fell on them, and they knew that it was because of our god that this work was finished. In those days letters came to Tobiah from many nobles of Judah, and those of Tobiah came to them. For many in Judah were bound to him by oath, because he was the son-in-law of Shekaniah ben Arah, and Johanan his son had taken the daughter of Meshullam ben Berechiah as wife. They reported his words to me and told my words to him, and Tobiah sent letters to terrify me.

2nd Ezra: Chapter 16 Notes

1 Codex Vaticanus: Ônô (ѡＮѡ)

- Aleppo Codex: Åwnw (אונו)

- Leningrad Codex: Ovnov (אֹונֹו)

The plains of Ono was the Canaanite name of the region approximately 11 kilometers (6.8 miles) east of Jaffa, towards Jerusalem.

2 Codex Vaticanus: Eloul (ЄλOΥλ)

- Aleppo Codex: Ålwl (אלול)

- Leningrad Codex: Elul (אֱלוּל)

Elul is the sixth month in the Hebrew Ecclesiastical calendar. The Hebrew Calendar is a lunisolar calendar, and so the months move somewhat in comparison to the Gregorian Calendar, and therefore the equivalent could be anywhere between August and September, depending on the year. However, Elul falls before the Northern Summer Solstice, and therefore September is the likely month being referenced.

2nd Ezra: Chapter 17

When the wall was built, and I had set up the doors, and the porters and the singers and the Levites were appointed, I placed in charge Hananiah my brother, and Hananiah the ruler of the palace[1] over Jerusalem, for he was a true man, and one that feared God beyond many other.

I said to them, "The gates of Jerusalem will not be opened until sunrise, and while they are still watching, let the doors be shut and bolted, and set watches from those who live in Jerusalem, every man at his post, and every man near his house."

The city was wide and large, and the people were few in it, and the houses were not rebuilt. God put it into my heart, and I gathered the nobles, and the rulers, and the people, into companies, and I found a register of the company that came up originally, and I found written in it as follows:[2] "These are the sons of the country, that came up from the colony, of the number which King Nebuchadnezzar of Babylon took away, and they returned to Jerusalem and Judah, each man to his city, with Zerubbabel, Jesus, Nehemiah, Azariah, Raamiah, Nahamani, Mordecai, Bilshan, Mispereth, Ezra, Bigvai, Nehum, Baanah, Mizpar, men of the people of Israel.

Sons of Pharez: 2172.

Sons of Shephatiah: 372.

Sons of Arah: 652.

Sons of Pahathmoab: with the sons of Jesus and Joab: 2818.

Sons of Elam: 1254.

Sons of Zattu: 845.

Sons of Zaccai: 760.

Sons of Bani: 648.

Sons of Bebai: 628.

Sons of Azgad: 2322.

Sons of Adonikam: 667.

Sons of Bigvai: 2067.

Sons of Adin: 655.

Sons of Ater: ben Hezekiah: 98.

Sons of Hashum: 328.

Sons of Bezai: 324.

Sons of Hariph: 112.

Sons of Gibeon: 95.

Sons of Bethlehem: 123.

Sons of Netophah: 56.

Sons of Anathoth: 128.

Men of Beth Azmaveth: 42.

Men of Kirjathjearim, Chephirah, and Beeroth: 743.

Men of Ramah and Geba: 621.

Men of Michmas: 122.

Men of Bethel and Ai: 123.

Men of the other Nebo:³ 52.

Men of the other Elam: 1254.

Men of Harim: 320.

Sons of Jericho: 345.

Sons of Lod, Adid, and Ono: 721.

Sons of Senaah: 3930.

The priests: the sons of Jedaiah, in the temple of Jesus: 973.

The sons of Immer: 1052.

The sons of Pashur: 1247.

The sons of Harim: 1017.

The Levites: the sons of Jesus of Kadmiel, with the sons of Hodevah: 74.

The singers, the sons of Asaph: 148.

The porters, the sons of Shallum, Ater, Talmon, Akkub, Hatita, and Shobai: 138.

The Nethins, the sons of Ziha, the sons of Hashupha, the sons of Tabbaoth, the sons of Keros, the sons of Sia, the sons of Padon, the sons of Lebana, the sons of Hagaba, the sons of Shalmai, the sons of Hanan, the sons of Giddel, the sons of Gahar, the sons of Reaiah, the sons of Rezin, the sons of Nekoda, the sons of Gazzam, the sons of Uzza, the sons of Phaseah, the sons of Bezai, the sons of Meunim, the sons of Nephishesim, the sons of Bakbuk, the sons of Achipha, the sons of Harhur, the sons of Bazlith, the sons of Mehida, the sons of Harsha, the sons of Barkos, the sons of Sisera, the sons of Tamah, the sons of Neziah, and the sons of Hatipha.

The sons of the servants of Solomon, the sons of Sotai, the sons of Sophereth, the sons of Perida, the sons of Jaala, the sons of Darkon, the sons of Giddel, the sons of Shephatiah, the sons of Hattil, the sons of Pochereth, the sons of Zebaim, the sons of Amon.

All the Nethins, and sons of the servants of Solomon, were 392.

These traveled from Tel Melah, Tel Harasha, Cherub, Eron, Immer, but they could not declare the houses of their families, or their seed, whether they were of Israel.

The sons of Delaiah, the sons of Tobiah, the sons of Nekoda: 642.

Of the priests: the sons of Habaiah, the sons of Koz, the sons of Barzillai, who they took wives of the daughters of Barzillai the Gileadite, and were called by his name. These searched for the genealogy of their family, and it was not found, and they were expelled from the priesthood. The military commander said they should not eat from the holy of holies, until a priest should rise to shed light on it.

All the congregation was about 42,360, besides their man-slaves and woman-slaves, these were 7337, and the singing-men and singing-women were 245, and there were 2700 donkeys."

Some of the heads of families gave into the treasury to Nehemiah for the work, a thousand pieces of gold, fifty bowls, and thirty priests' garments. Some of the heads of families gave into the treasuries of the work, twenty thousand pieces of gold, and two thousand and three hundred pounds of silver. The rest of the people gave twenty thousand pieces of gold, and two thousand and two hundred pounds of silver, and sixty-seven priests' garments. The priests, and Levites, and porters, and singers, and some of the people, and the Nethins, and all Israel, lived in their cities.

2nd Ezra: Chapter 17 Notes

1 The Septuagint uses the same name twice: Anania (Aναvια), while the Masoretic text list them as Chanani (חֲנָנִי) and Chananyah (חֲנַנְיָה). The names are separated in with 'and' (καὶ) in Greek, and with 'and you' (וְאֶת) in the transliterated Aramaic found in the Masoretic text.

The Aramaic sentence structure implies that this may have originally been part of a letter to Nehemiah's brother Hanani about the appointment of Hananiah, however, neither the Septuagint nor Masoretic Text are clear at this point, and so the text of the Septuagint is followed, with the name Hananiah used, as it is the Aramaic and Hebrew form of Aναvια.

2 The following register of families dates back to the original group that returned from Babylon during the reign of Cyrus II, circa 539 BC. It is a similar list to the one found in chapter 2, and 1st Ezra chapter 5, however, none of the lists match in the Septuagint, and the lists in chapters 2 and 17 this book do not match in the Masoretic text, proving that the Nehemiah section of 2nd Ezra was a separate work before being merged with Ezra.

The merger must have taken place before the Septuagint was translated into Greek, and before the Hebrew translation was made, as both versions are essentially the same.

3 Codex Vaticanus: Nabi - aar (ⲚⲀⲂⲒ-ⲀⲀⲣ)

• Aleppo Codex: Nbw åḥr (נבו אחר). Translation: Nebo the other

• Leningrad Codex: Nevov acher (נְבוֹ אַחֵר). Translation: Nebo the other

As the Greeks appear to have transliterated åḥr as aar, the meaning is restored from the Masoretic text.

2nd Ezra: Chapter 18

The seventh month arrived, and the Israelites were settled in their cities, and all the people were gathered as one man to the broad place before the water-gate, and they told Ezra the scribe to bring the book of the law of Moses, which the Lord commanded to Israel. So Ezra the priest brought the law before the congregation both of men and women, and everyone who had understanding was present to listen, on the first day of the seventh month. He read it from the time of sunrise to midday, before the men and the women, and they understood it, and the ears of all the people were attentive to the book of the law.

Ezra the scribe stood on a wooden stage, and next to him stood Mattithiah, Shema, Hananiah, Uriah, Hachaliah, and Maaseiah on his right hand, and on his left were Pedaiah, Mishael, Malchiah, Hushim, Hashbadana, Zachariah, and Meshullam. Ezra opened the book before all the people, for he was above the people, and it happened that when he had opened it, all the people stood up.

Ezra blessed the Lord, the greatest god, and all the people replied, "Amen," lifting their hands, and they bowed down and worshiped the Lord with their face to the ground.

Jesus, Bani, and Sherebiah instructed the people in the law, and the people stood in their place. They read in the book of the law of God, and Ezra taught and instructed them distinctly in the knowledge of the Lord, and the people understood the law in the reading. Nehemiah and Ezra the priest and scribe, and the Levites, and those that instructed the people spoke and said to all the people, "It is a holy day to our Lord God. Do not mourn or cry," as all the people wept when they heard the words of the law.

The governor said to them, "Go, eat the fat, and drink the sweet, and give portions to those that have nothing, for the day is holy to the Lord. Don't faint, that which exists is powerful."

The Levites made the people silent, saying, "Be silent! It is a holy day, and don't be sad," so all the people departed to eat, and to drink, and to send portions, and celebrated, for they understood the words which he made known to them.

On the second day the heads of families assembled with all the people, also the priests and Levites, with Ezra the scribe, to listen to all the words of the law. They found written in the law which the Lord commanded Moses, that the Israelites should live in huts in the feast in the seventh month, and that they should sound with trumpets in all their cities, and in Jerusalem.

Ezra said, "Go out to the mountain, and bring olive branches, and branches from cypress trees, and branches of myrtle, and branches of palm trees, and branches of every thick tree, to make huts, as it was written."

The people went out, and brought them, and made huts for themselves, each one on his roof, and in their courts, and in the courts of the Temple of God, and in the streets of the city, and as far as the gate of Ephraim. All the congregation who had returned from the colony made huts, and lived in huts, for the Israelites had not done so from the days of Joshua ben Nun until that day, and there was a great celebration.

Ezra read from the book of the law of God daily, from the first day even to the last day, and they kept the feast seven days, and on the eighth day, there was a solemn assembly, following the ordinance.

2ⁿᵈ Ezra: Chapter 19

On the twenty-fourth day of the month, the Israelites assembled with fasting, wearing sackcloth, and with ashes on their head. The Israelites separated themselves from every foreigner, and stood and confessed their sins and the iniquities of their fathers. They stood in their place, and read in the book of the law of their Lord God, and they confessed their sins to the Lord, and worshiped their Lord God.

On the stairs stood, from the Levites: Jesus and the sons of Kadmiel, Shechaniah ben Sherebiah the sons of Chenani, and they cried with a loud voice to their Lord God. The Levites, Jesus, and Kadmiel said, "Rise up, bless our Lord God forever and ever! Let them bless your glorious name, and exalt it with all blessing and praise."

Ezra said, "You are the only true god! You made the sky, and the sky of the sky, and all their array, the earth, and all things that are in it, the seas, and all things in them, and you quicken all things, and the armies of the sky worship you. You are the Lord God. You chose Abram, and brought him out of the land of the Chaldeans, and gave him the name of Abraham! You found his heart faithful before you and made a covenant with him to give to him and to his descendants the land of the Canaanites, and the Greeks,[1] and Amorites, and Perizzite, and Jebusites, and Girgashites."

"You have confirmed your words, for you are right-eous. You saw the affliction of our fathers in Egypt, and you heard their cry at the Papyrus Sea.² You showed signs and wonders in Egypt, to Pharaoh and all his servants, and on all the people of his land, for you know that they behaved insolently against them, and you made yourself a name, as like today. You divided the sea before them, and they passed through the middle of the sea on dry land, and you threw into the deep, those that were about to pursue them, like a stone in the mighty water. You guided them by day by a pillar of cloud, and by night by a pillar of fire, to show them how they should walk."

"Also you came down on Mount Sinai, and you spoke to them out of the sky, and gave them right judgments, and laws of truth, ordinances, and good commandments. You made known to them your holy sabbath. You gave them commandments, and ordinances, and a law, by the hand of your servant Moses. You gave them bread from the sky for their food, and you brought them water from a rock for their thirst, and you commanded them to go in to inherit the land over which you stretched out your hand to give it to them. But they and our fathers behaved proudly, and hardened their neck, and did not listen to your commandments, and refused to listen, and did not remember your wonders which you worked with them, and they hardened their neck, and appointed a leader to return to their slavery in Egypt."

"But you, God, are merciful and compassionate, long-suffering, and generous in mercy, and you did not abandon them. Still, they made for themselves a molten calf, and said, "These are the gods that brought us out of Egypt, and they worked great provocations. Yet you in your great compassion did not abandon them in the wilderness, you remove from them the pillar of the cloud by day, to guide them along the path, nor the pillar of fire at night, to illuminate for them where they should walk. You gave your good spirit to instruct them, and you did not withhold your manna from their mouth and gave them water in their thirst. You sustained them forty years in the wilderness, you did not allow anything to fail them, their garments did not grow old, and their feet were not bruised."

"Moreover, you gave them kingdoms, and divided the nations to them, and they inherited the land of Sihon king of Heshbon, and the land of Og king of Bashan. You multiplied their children like the stars of the sky and brought them into the land of which you promised to their fathers. They inherited it, and you destroyed before them the residents in the land of the Canaanites, and you gave them into their hands, and their kings, and the nations of the land, to do to them as it pleased them."

"They took mighty cities, and inherited houses full of all good things, wells dug, vineyards, and olive yards, and every fruit tree in abundance, and so they ate, and were filled, and grew fat, and celebrated in your great goodness. But they turned, and revolted from you, and threw way your law, and they killed your prophets, who testified against them to turn them back to you, and they worked great provocations. Then you gave them into the hand of those that afflicted them, and they did afflict them, and they cried to you in the time of their affliction, and you did hear them from your abode in the sky, and in your great compassion gave them deliverers, and did save them from the hand of those who afflicted them."

"When they rested, they did evil again before you, so you left them in the hands of their enemies, and they ruled over them, and they cried again to you, and you heard them from the sky, and delivered them in your great compassion. You testified against them, to bring them back to your law, but they did not listen, and sinned against your commandments and your judgments, which if a man does, he will live in them, and they turned their back, and hardened their neck, and did not listen. Yet you were patient with them many years, and testified to them by your spirit by the hand of your prophets, but they did not listen, so you gave them into the hand of the nations of the land. But you, in your many mercies, did not appoint them to destruction, and did not abandon them, for you are strong, and merciful, and pitiful."

"Now, our god, the powerful, the great, the mighty, and the terrible, keeping your covenant and your mercy, don't let all the trouble seem little in your sight that has come on us, and our kings, and our princes, and our priests, and our prophets, and our fathers, and on all your people, from the days of the kings of Assyria even until today. You are righteous in all the things that come on us, for you have worked faithfully, but we have greatly sinned. Our kings, and our princes, and our priests, and our fathers, have not followed your law, and have not paid attention to your commandments, and have not kept your testimonies which you testified to them. They did not serve you in your kingdom, and in your great goodness which you gave to them, and in the large and fat land which you did furnish before them, and they turned not from their evil devices."

"Look, we are servants today, and as for the land which you gave to our fathers to eat the fruit from it and the good things from it, look, we are servants on it, and its produce is abundant for the kings whom you appointed over us because of our sins, and they have dominion over our bodies, and over our livestock, as it pleases them, and we are in great affliction. Regarding all these circumstances we make a covenant, and write it, and our princes, our Levites, and our priests, set their seal to it."

2nd Ezra: Chapter 19 Notes

1 Codex Vaticanus: Chettaion (ΧΕΤΤΑΙѠΝ)

- Aleppo Codex: Hty (חתי). Translation: Cypriots (or Greeks)

- Leningrad Codex: Chitti (חִתִּי). Translation: Cypriots (or Greeks)

This term has created a great deal of confusion since the misidentification of the ruins of the Neshites as being 'Hittite' in the 1800s. The modern archaeological name 'Hittite,' is not derived from an ancient name for the culture applied by themselves, or anyone else, but rather adopted from the biblical reference to a then-unknown civilization somewhere in the region. There was an ancient culture in the region called the Hattians, however, they were conquered by the Nesites before 1700 BC, and subsequently disappeared from the historic records.

The name was applied to culture today referred to as 'Hittites,' before the 'Hittite' language had been translated, and is incorrect. Since 1906, excavations at Boğazköy, the ancient 'Hittite' capital Hattusa have uncovered more than 10,000 'Hittite' texts, including the royal achieve. The actual name of the 'Hittite' language and people was Nešili (𒉈𒅆𒇷), which is now rendered in some academic literate as Nesite or Neshite.

As early as the mid-1800s some scholars disputed the identification of the Nesites as the Biblical Hittites, including the Orientalist Max Müller, who was one of many claiming the Biblical Hittites were ancient Greeks or some other Mediterranean people. Later in the Septuagint's translation of the Maccabees, the similar term Chettiim (Χεττιιμ) as a reference to all Greek-speaking lands.

In the 1st century AD, the Jewish historian Josephus reported that Cethima was the name of Cyrus in Aramaic, and the Chettim were the descendants of Noah's grandson Chethimus, who had settled on Cyprus. Josephus reported that the name was preserved in the Greek name of the town Cition (Κίτιον).

Most historians view it as more likely that the Aramaic name was derived from the city-state of Cition, which was known as Kåtjåy (𓈖𓐠𓈖𓏏𓇌) in Egyptian records from the New Kingdom Era in the late Bronze Age, and Kt (𐤕𐤊) or Kty (𐤕𐤊𐤉) in Phoenician records from the early Iron Age. While this may be the origin of the term, by the era of the Neo-Assyrian era, the term must have also referred to other Greek islands, as both the prophets Isaiah and Ezekiel used the term 'Islands of Kittim.' As the term referred to all Greek lands in Aramaic by the time of Ezekiel, the translations of 'Greece' and 'Greeks' are used here.

2 Codex Vaticanus: Erythran thalassan (ⲉⲣⲩⲑⲣⲁⲛ ⲑⲁⲗⲁⲥⲥⲁⲛ). Translation: Erythrean Sea

• Aleppo Codex: ym swp (יַם סוף). Translation: sea of reeds (or papyrus)

• Leningrad Codex: yam-suf (יַם־סוּף). Translation: sea of reeds (or papyrus)

The Codex Vaticanus' Book of Judges maintains the Greek transliteration of the name the Suf (סוּף) Sea as Siph (Σιφ) Sea, while the later Codex Alexandrinus uses the more common Greek translation of Erythrean (Ἐρυθρᾶσ) Sea. The confirms that the Aramaic text the Greeks translated used the name Swf Sea.

Both the Aramaic swf (ܣܘܦ) and Canaanite term swf (𐤎𐤅𐤐), meaning papyrus plants, were adopted from the Egyptian term tjufi (𓇋𓆑𓏤), which referred to papyrus, papyrus plants, and papyrus marshes. The Egyptian term continued to be used into the Classical era as the Coptic words čoouf (ϫⲟⲟⲩϥ), conf (ϭⲟⲛϥ), and comf (ϭⲟⲙϥ), all meaning papyrus. Conversely, the Egyptian name of the Red Sea was the Sea of Heh (𓎛), meaning 'very large sea' from the Middle Kingdom era onward, however, it is believed to have originally been named after the ancient Egyptian frog god Heh (𓏏𓏏𓆐). As the Greek translation of Erythrean Sea is anachronistic, the translation of Papyrus Sea is imported from the Masoretic Text.

2nd Ezra: Chapter 20

On the seal, were Nehemiah (the military commander,) son of Hachaliah,[1] and Zidkijah ben Seraiah, and Azariah, Jeremiah, Phasur, Amariah, Malchiah, Hattush, Shebani, Malouch, Iram, Meremoth, Obadiah, Daniel, Ginnethon, Baruch, Meshullam, Abijah, Miniamin, Maaziah, Bilgai, and Shemaiah. These were priests.

The Levites: Jesus ben Azaniah, Binnui of the sons of Henadad, Kadmiel and his brothers, Shebaniah, Hodijah, Kelita, Pelaiah, Hanan, Micha, Rehob, Hashabiah, Zaccur, Sherebiah, Shebaniah, Odum the sons of Beninu.

The heads of the people: Parosh, Pahathmoab, Elam, Zattu, the sons of Bani, Azgad, Bebai, Adonijah, Bigvai, Adin Ater, Hizkijah, Azzur, Hodijah, Hashum, Bezai, Hariph, Anathoth, Nebai, Magpiash, Mesullam, Hezir, Meshezabeel, Zadok, Jaddua, Pelatiah, Hanan, Hananiah, Hoshea, Hananiah, Hashub, Hallohesh, Pileha, Shobek, Rehum, Hashabnah, Maaseiah, Ahijah, Heman, Anan, Malluch, Harim, and Baanah.

The rest of the people, the priests, the Levites, the porters, the singers, the Nethins, and everyone who drew off from the nations of the land to the law of God, their wives, their sons, their daughters, everyone who had knowledge and understanding, were urgent with their brothers, and bound them under a curse, and entered into a curse, and into an oath, to walk in the law of God, which was given by the hand of Moses, the servant of God, to keep and to do all the commandments of the Lord, and his judgments, and his ordinances, in that "We will not", they said, "give our daughters to the people of the land, nor will we take their daughters for our sons. As for the people of the land who offer wares and all merchandise for sale on the sabbath-day, we will not buy from them on the sabbath or the holy day, and we will leave the seventh year, and the exaction of every debt. We will impose ordinances on ourselves, to levy on ourselves a third of a shekel annually for the service of the temple of our god, the showbread, and the continual meat-offering, and for the continual whole burnt offering, of the sabbaths, of the new moon, for the feast, and for the holy things, and the sin-offering, to make atonement for Israel, and for the works of the temple of our god."

We cast lots for the office of wood-bearing, we the priests, and the Levites, and the people, to bring wood into the house of our god, according to the house of our families, at certain set times, year by year, to burn on the altar of our Lord God, as it is written in the law, and to bring the first-fruits of our land, and the first-fruits of the fruit of every tree, year by year, into the Temple of the Lord, the firstborn of our sons, and of our livestock, as it is written in the law, and the firstborn of our herds and of our flocks, to bring to the temple of our god, for the priests that minister in the temple of our god.

The first-fruits of our grain, and the fruit of every tree, of wine, and of oil, we will bring to the priests to the treasury of the Temple of God, and a tithe of our land to the Levites, as the Levites themselves will receive tithes in all the cities of the land we cultivate. The priests, the sons of Aaron will be with the Levites in the tithe of the Levites, and the Levites will bring up the tenth part of their tithe to the temple of our god, into the treasuries of the Temple of God. For the Israelites and the sons of Levi will bring into the treasuries the first-fruits of the grain, and wine, and oil, and there are the holy vessels, and the priests, and the ministers, and the porters, and the singers, and we will not abandon the temple of our god.

2ⁿᵈ Ezra: Chapter 20 Notes

1 Codex Vaticanus: Neemias uios Achalia (ΝΕΕΜΙΑΣ ΥΙΟΣ ΑΧΑΛΙΑ). Translation: Nehemiah son of Hachaliah

- Aleppo Codex: Nḥmyh htrštå bn ḥklyh (נחמיה התרשתא בן חכליה). Translation: Nechemyah the military commander son of Chachalyah

- Leningrad Codex: Nechemyah hattirshata ben-Chachalyah (נְחֶמְיָה הַתִּרְשָׁתָא בֶּן־חֲכַלְיָה). Translation: Nechemyah the military commander son of Chachalyah

Nehemiah ben Hachaliah, is the Nehemiah who was sent to Jerusalem in the twentieth year of a King Artaxerxes reign, and is in this verse present during the seventh year of another Artaxerxes reign, proving that the kings in question were Artaxerxes II and III. While it is unclear how old Nehemiah was when Artaxerxes II sent him to Jerusalem, it is clear he was an adult, likely between 20 and 40 years of age, and that was in Artaxerxes II's 20ᵗʰ year, which was 384 BC. Artaxerxes III inherited the throne in 358 BC, and sent Ezra to Jerusalem in his 7ᵗʰ year, which was 351 BC.

This means that it had been 33 years since Nehemiah returned to Jerusalem to rebuild the walls, and he would have likely been between 53 and 73 years old. Earlier it was reported that he worked as the 'governor' until the 32ⁿᵈ year of Artaxerxes, which has to be Artaxerxes II, and would have been 372 BC, later it is reported that after that time he returned to the king, but after some time returned to Jerusalem, apparently now as the military commander, likely before his patron Artaxerxes II died in 358 BC.

The word used in the Masoretic Text, is rendered as Attharias (Ατθαριας) in other sections of the Septuagint. It is generally interpreted as meaning something like 'governor' in translations of the Masoretic Text, however, it is not the Hebrew, Aramaic, Persian, or Babylonian word for 'governor.' The Persian word for governor, xšaçapāvan (𒀭𒍝𒄩𒄩𒀀𒄿𒂊𒄩) is transliterated in the Hebrew version of Esther as achashdarpan (אֲחַשְׁדַּרְפָּן), which makes hattirshata (הַתִּרְשָׁתָא) an unlikely transliteration. The word that the author was likely trying to transliterate, was the Persian word artshtaran (ارتشـتاران) which translates as military 'chieftain.'

2nd Ezra: Chapter 21

The chiefs of the people lived in Jerusalem, and the rest of the people cast lots, to bring one of every ten to live in Jerusalem the holy city, and the other nine in the other cities. The people blessed all the men that volunteered to live in Jerusalem. Now, these are the chiefs of the province who lived in Jerusalem, and the cities of Judah. Every man lived on his possession in their cities in Israel, the priests, and the Levites, and the Nethins, and the sons of the servants of Solomon. Both Judahites and Benjaminites lived in Jerusalem.

From the Judahites: Athaiah ben Uzziah ben Zechariah ben Meraiah ben Shephatiah ben Mahalaleel of the sons of Pharez, and Maaseiah ben Baruch ben Colhozeh ben Hazaiah ben Adaiah ben Joiarib ben Zachariah ben Shiloni. All the sons of Pharez who lived in Jerusalem were four hundred and sixty-eight mighty men.

These were the Benjaminites: Shiloh ben Meshullam ben Joed ben Pedaiah ben Kolaiah ben Maaseiah ben Ithiel ben Jesaiah. Following him were Gabbai, Sallai, and 928, Joel been Zichri commanded them, and Judah ben Senuah was second in the city.

From the priests: both Jedaiah ben Joiarib, and Jachin, Zerahiah ben Hachaliah ben Meshullam ben Zadok ben Meraioth ben Ahitub was in charge of the Temple of

God. Their brothers doing the work of the temple were 822.

Adaiah ben Jeroham ben Pelaliah ben Amzi ben Zechariah ben Pashur ben Malchiah, and his brothers, chiefs of families, were 242.

Amashai ben Azareel ben Meshillemoth ben Immer, and his brothers, mighty warriors, were 128, commanded by Badiel, ben great men.

From the Levites: Shemaiah ben Esricam, Mattaniah ben Micha, and Jobeb ben Samui, and 284.

The porters: Akkub, Talmon, and their brothers, were 172.

The overseer of the Levites was ben Bani ben Uzza ben Hashabiah ben Micha.

From the sons of Asaph the singers, some were in charge of the Temple of God, following the king's commandment regarding them. Pethahiah ben Baseza attended on behalf of the king for every matter of the people, and in regards to the villages in their country district.

Some of the Judahites lived in Kirjath Arba, and in Jesus, and in Beersheba, and their villages, Lachish and its countryside, and they pitched their tents in Beersheba.

The Benjaminites lived from Geba to Michmash.

From the Levites, there were divisions in Judah and Benjamin.

2nd Ezra: Chapter 22

Now, these are the priests and the Levites that traveled with Zerubbabel ben Shealtiel, and Jesus: Zerahiah, Jeremiah, Ezra, Meraiah, Malluch, Shechaniah. These were the chiefs of the priests and their brothers in the days of Jesus:

The Levites were: Jesus, Bani, Kadmiel, Sherebiah, Jedaiah, and Mattaniah. He was over the bands, and his brothers were appointed to the daily schedules. Jesus fathered Joakim, and Joakim fathered Eliashib, and Eliashib fathered Jedaiah, and Jedaiah fathered Jonathan, and Jonathan fathered Jaddua.

In the days of Joakim, his brothers the priests, and the heads of families:

of Zerahiah: Meraiah,

of Jeremiah: Hananiah,

of Ezra: Meshullam,

of Amariah: Johanan,

of Melicu: Jonathan,

of Shebaniah: Joseph,

of Are: Mannas,

of Meraioth: Helkai,

of Iddo: Zechariah,

of Ginnethon: Meshullam,

of Abijah: Zichri,

of Miniamin: Moadiah,

of Piltai, of Bilgah: Shammua,

of Shemaiah: Jonathan,

of Joiarib: Mattaniah,

of Edio: Uzzi,

of Sallai: Kallai,

of Amok: Eber,

of Hachaliah: Hashabiah,

and of Jedaiah: Nethaneel.

The Levites in the days of Eliashib, Joiada, Johanan, and Jaddua, were recorded heads of families, and were also the priests, in the reign of Darius the Persian.

The Levites: heads of families, were recorded in the Book of Paralipomena,[1] even to the days of Johanan son of Elishua. The heads of the Levites were Hashabiah, Sherebiah, Jesus, and the sons of Kadmiel, and their brothers with them were to sing hymns of praise, according to the commandment of David the prophet, course by course.

When I gathered the porters in the days of Joakim ben Jesus ben Jehozadak, and in the days of Nehemiah,² Ezra the priest was the scribe. At the dedication of the wall of Jerusalem, they wanted the Levites in their places, to bring them to Jerusalem, to keep a feast of dedication and joy with thanksgiving, and they played cymbals with songs and had lutes and harps. The sons of the singers were assembled from the neighborhood around Jerusalem, and from the villages, and the country, as the singers built themselves villages near Jerusalem.

The priests and the Levites purified themselves, and they purified the people, and the porters, and the wall. They brought up the princes of Judah on the wall, and they appointed two great companies for thanksgiving, and they passed on the right hand on the wall of the dung-gate. Following them were Hoshaiah, and half the princes of Judea, and Azariah, Ezra, Meshullam, Judah, Benjamin, Shemaiah, and Jeremiah.

Some of the sons of the priest had trumpets, Zachariah ben Jonathan ben Shemaiah ben Mattaniah ben Michaiah ben Zaccur ben Asaph, and his brothers, Shemaiah, Azarael, Gilalai, Jama, Ahijah, Nethaneel, Judah, and Hananiah, and praised with the hymns of David the prophet. Ezra the scribe was leading them at the gate, praising ahead of them and they went up by the steps of the City of David, in the ascent of the wall, above the house of David, all the way to the water-gate of Ephraim, and to the fish-gate, and by the tower of Hananeel, and as far as the sheep-gate. The singers were heard and were counted.

On that day they offered great sacrifices, and rejoiced, for God had made them very joyful, and their wives and their children rejoiced, and the joy in Jerusalem was heard from far away. On that day they appointed men over the treasuries, for the treasures, the first-fruits, and the tithes, and for the chiefs of the cities who were assembled among them, to furnish portions for the priests and Levites, for there was joy in Judah over the priests and over the Levites that waited. They followed the orders of their God, and the ordinances for purification, and organized the singers and the porters according to the commandments of David and his son Solomon, as in the days of David, Asaph was originally the first of the singers, and they sang hymns and praise to God.

All Israel in the days of Zerubbabel, and the days of Nehemiah, gave the portions of the singers and the porters, a daily rate, and consecrated them to the Levites, and the Levites consecrated them to the sons of Aaron.

2nd Ezra: Chapter 22 Notes

1 Codex Vaticanus: bibliô logôn tôn hêmerôn (ⲃⲓⲃⲗⲓⲱ ⲗⲟⲅⲱⲛⲧⲱⲛⲏⲙⲉⲣⲱⲛ). Translation: Book of the Words of the Days

• Aleppo Codex: spr dbry hymym (ספר דברי הימים). Translation: book of the words of the days

• Leningrad Codex: sefer divrei hayyamim (סֵפֶר דִּבְרֵי הַיָּמִים). Translation: book of the words of the days

The Greek name of the book is a literally translation of the name of the books that ended up being called 1st and 2nd Paralipomenon in the Septuagint, meaning Ezra must have been translated before the Paralipomena, which are themselves are generally accepted as being translated circa 200 BC.

2 Codex Vaticanus: Neemia (ⲛⲉⲉⲙⲓⲁ). Translation: Nehemiah

• Aleppo Codex: nhmyh hphh (נחמיה הפחה). Translation: Nehemiah the lesser (or younger)

• Leningrad Codex: Nechemyah happechah (נְחֶמְיָה הַפֶּחָה). Translation: Nehemiah the lesser (or younger)

The Masoretic version of the text implies that the Nehemiah in the time of Ezra was a different Nehemiah that the former governor, who is most likely the author of this section of text. The entire section of text continues consistently into chapter 23, which is certainty written from Nehemiah's viewpoint. If there was another word in the

Aramaic version of Ezra-Nehemiah, the Greeks would have transliterated it if they did not understand it, implying the word was added when the Hebrew version was translated. The sentence structure is quite different between the Greek and Hebrew versions, as the Greek is written from someone's perspective who was most-likely Nehemiah, while in the Hebrew translation, the perspective is dropped, and this is simply a statement of people that were present at the time.

As there was no reason to clarify that this Nehemiah was not the author speaking in the third person if it was not in his perspective, this appears to have been in the text before the Hebrew translation was made, which suggests this was a scribal note in the Aramaic Book of Ezra-Nehemiah that the Greek translators did not translate, and therefore it is added to this translation in parentheses.

2nd Ezra: Chapter 23

On the day they read from the book of Moses to the ears of the people, it was found written in it, that the Ammonites and Moabites should not enter into the congregation of God forever, because they did not meet the Israelites with bread and water, but hired Balaam against them to curse them, but our god turned the curse into a blessing. When they heard the law, they separated all the foreigners from Israel.

Before this time, Eliashib the priest lived in the treasury of the temple of our god, who was connected to Tobiah, and he made a great treasury for himself. There, they were formerly in the habit of giving the offerings, and the frankincense, and the vessels, and the tithe of the grain, and the wine, and the oil, the commanded portion of the Levites, and singers, and porters, and the first-fruits of the priests. In all this time, I was not in Jerusalem, for in the thirty-second year of King Artaxerxes of Babylon I returned to the king, and after some time I made my request of the king, and I returned to Jerusalem, and I understood the evil which Eliashib had done with Tobiah, in making for himself a treasury in the court of the Temple of God.

It seemed very evil to me, so I threw out all the furniture of the house of Tobiah from the treasury. I gave orders, and they purified the treasuries, and I returned to there the vessels of the Temple of God, and the offerings, and the frankincense. I understood that the portion of the Levites had not been given, and they had fled, each one to his field, both Levites and the singers, that were supposed to be doing the work. I argued with the commanders, and said, "Why has the Temple of God been abandoned?" and I assembled them, and put them in their place.

All Judah brought a tithe of the wheat and the wine and the oil into the treasuries, into the charge of Shelemiah the priest, and Zadok the scribe, and Pedaiah of the Levites, and next to them was Hanan ben Zaccur ben Mattaniah, for they were considered faithful. It was their office to distribute to their brothers. Remember me, God, in this, and don't let my kindness be forgotten which I have worked regarding the Temple of the Lord God.

In those days I saw in Judea men treading wine presses on the sabbath and carrying sheaves, and loading donkeys with wine, grapes, figs, and other burdens, and bringing them into Jerusalem on the sabbath-day, and I testified in the day of their sale. Also, there were those living there bringing fish, and selling every kind of merchandise to the Judahites in Jerusalem on the sabbath. I argued with the free Judahites, and said to them, "What is this evil that you do, to profane the sabbath-day? Didn't your fathers do this, and our God brought on them, and on us, and on this city, all these evils? Do you bring additional anger on Israel by profaning the sabbath?"

While the gates were opened in Jerusalem before the sabbath that I spoke, they shut the gates, I ordered that they should not be opened until after the sabbath. I set some of my servants at the gates, that none should bring in burdens on the sabbath-day. So all the merchants lodged and carried on business outside of Jerusalem once or twice, and then I chastised them, saying, "Why do you lodge outside of the wall? If you do so again, I will stretch out my hand against you."

From that time, they did not come on the sabbath, and I told the Levites who were purifying themselves, and came and kept the gates, that they should sanctify the sabbath-day.

Remember me, God, for these things, and spare me according to the abundance of your mercy.

In those days I saw the Judahites who had married women of Ashdod, Amman, and Moab, and their children spoke half in the language of Ashdod, and did not know how to speak in the Judahite language. I chased and cursed them, and I hit some of them, and pulled their hair, and made them swear by God, saying, "You will not give your daughters to their sons, and you will not take their daughters for your sons. Didn't King Solomon of Israel sin like this? Though there was no king like him among many nations, and he was beloved of God, and God made him king over all Israel, yet foreign women turned him away. So we will not allow you to do this evil, to break covenant with our god and marry foreign wives!"

I chased away from me Eliashib the high priest, one of the sons of Joiada, being the son-in-law of Sanballat the Aaronite.

Remember them, God, for their false connection with the priesthood, and breaking the covenant of the priesthood, and for defiling the Levites.

I purged them from all foreign connections and established schedules for the priests and the Levites, every man according to his work. The offering of the wood-bearers was at certain set times, and in the times of the first-fruits.

Remember me, God, as good.

Septuagint Manuscripts

The following is a list of the Septuagint manuscripts referenced in the notes for this book.

LXX B (Codex Vaticanus) is dated to the 4th century. It is currently located at the Vatican Library (Gr. 1209 in Vatican City.

Alternative Translations

The following is a list of alternative translations that were used for comparative analysis.

The Aleppo Codex is dated to circa 920 AD. For centuries it was housed at the Central Synagogue of Aleppo, from which its name is derived. It was the oldest known complete copy of the Hebrew scriptures used within Judaism until 1947, when it was seized and divided among Jewish families during anti-Jewish riots in Aleppo. The sections that have resurfaced are currently at the Israel Museum in Jerusalem. Approximately 40% is still missing.

The Leningrad Codex is dated to 1008 (or 1009 AD. It is currently located at the National Library of Russia (Firkovich B 19 A) in St. Petersburg. The Leningrad Codex is the oldest complete copy of the Hebrew scriptures used within Judaism.

Dead Sea Scrolls

The following is a list of the Dead Sea Scrolls mentioned in the notes for this book. Most are held by the Israel Museum in Jerusalem.

DSS 4Q117 (4QEzra) is dated to the Hasmonean dynasty in Judea (140 to 37 BC).

Also Available

SEPTUAGINT SERIES:

- Septuagint: Cosmic Genesis

- Septuagint: Exodus

- Septuagint: Leviticus

- Septuagint: Numbers

- Septuagint: Deuteronomy

- Septuagint: Joshua

- Septuagint: Judges and Ruth

- Septuagint: Kingdoms

- Septuagint: Paralipomena

- Septuagint: Ezra

- Septuagint: Tobit

- Septuagint: Judith

- Septuagint: Esther

- Septuagint: Maccabees

- Septuagint: Psalms and the Prayer of Manasseh

- Septuagint: Job

- Septuagint: Solomon

- Septuagint: Wisdom of Joshua ben Sira and Odes

- Septuagint: Torah

- Septuagint: History, Volume 1

- Septuagint: History, Volume 2

ALSO AVAILABLE

- Octateuch: The Original Orit

ENOCH AND METATRON SERIES:
- Books of Enoch Collection

- Books of Enoch and Metatron Collection

- Books of Metatron Collection

- Secrets of Enoch

OTHER TRANSLATIONS:
- Apocalypses of Ezra

- Arabic Maccabees

- Life of Adam and Eve

- Memories of the New Kingdom

- Septuagint's Esther and the Vetus Latina Esther

- Septuagint's Ezekiel and the Ba'al Cycle

- Septuagint's Job and the Testament of Job

- Septuagint's Proverbs and the Wisdom of Amenemope

- The Amarna Letters

- Testaments of the Patriarchs Collection

- Tobit and Ahikar

- Ugaritic Texts: Ba'al Cycle

- Wisdom of Ahikar

www.ingramcontent.com/pod-product-compliance
Lightning Source LLC
Chambersburg PA
CBHW061142120626
46546CB00005B/1896